horses

gabriele boiselle

WS White Star Publishers® is a registered
trademark property of De Agostini Libri S.p.A.

© 2006, 2013 De Agostini Libri S.p.A.
Via G. da Verrazano, 15
28100 Novara, Italy
www.whitestar.it - www.deagostini.it

Translation: Sarah Ponting

Revised Edition

ISBN 978-88-544-0725-1
  2 3 4 5 6   18 17 16 15 14

Printed in China

gabriele boiselle

horses

WHITE STAR PUBLISHERS

PHOTOGRAPHS
GABRIELE BOISELLE

TEXTS BY
GABRIELE BOISELLE
AGNÈS GALLETIER

project manager and editorial director
VALERIA MANFERTO DE FABIANIS

graphic designer
PAOLA PIACCO

editorial coordinator
GIADA FRANCIA

4-5   An affectionate moment between two Andalusian
stallions, which tenderly nuzzle, massage and nip each other.
Their majestic arching necks convey power, grace and love.

contents

6   The serious, gentle and deep eyes of horses always move me. They act like a mirror of ourselves, like a wise gaze resting on our sentimental hesitations, narrow mindedness and everything that so often prevent us from experiencing the moment to the full.

7   The feverish intensity of the horse's gaze, the graceful movement of its neck, its finely chiseled ears and velvety soft quivering nostrils all convey its sensitivity, untamed power and fragility.

9 left   Leaving the stables is an exciting moment, even for a Haflinger pony. The joy of unfettered movement for these

eternal comics is matched only by the pride of attracting the admiring gaze of onlookers.

9 center   Fear is never far away, especially for a mare and her foal, which she is always ready to defend from predators. It is essential to accept and know how to handle the visceral unease that often grips horses in order to photograph them and live with them.

9 right   The enchantment and admiration that we feel at the sight of a moving horse seem boundless. It's a universal emotion, which has united men since the dawn of time.

introduction

TAKING PHOTOGRAPHS MEANS SETTING OUR INNER GAZE ON THE OUTSIDE WORLD, SEEKING IN THE INTIMACY OF THE LENS THE MAGIC MOMENT IN WHICH THE TRUE IMAGE COINCIDES WITH OUR MOST HIDDEN FEELINGS.

GABRIELE BOISELLE'S FEELINGS FOR HORSES ARE STRONG, DEEP AND CONSTANTLY REKINDLED, ALWAYS CHARACTERIZED BY WONDER AND TENDERNESS, DESPITE THE MANY YEARS SPENT IN THEIR PRESENCE AND THE PURSUIT OF HER PROFESSION, WHICH COULD HAVE MADE THEM ORDINARY AND RATIONAL. SHE IS A PHOTOGRAPHER WITH A PASSIONATE LOVE FOR HORSES AND IS ABLE TO SENSE THEIR PERCEPTION OF THE WORLD AND FORESEE THEIR REACTIONS; SHE ALSO KNOWS HOW TO TALK TO THEM AND TOUCH THEM. SHE DEEPLY BREATHES IN AND ENJOYS THE SMELL OF STABLES AS OTHERS ENJOY THE SCENT OF A FLOWER. FEET IN THE DUNG OR MUD, SHE BURIES HER HANDS IN MANES, KISSES THE WARM AND VELVETY NOSES, HUGS ONE HORSE'S NECK, AND SCRATCHES ANOTHER'S EARS, RESTING HER HEAD ON ITS BACK AS THOUGH IT WERE A COMFORTING SHOULDER. SHE TALKS TO THE HORSES IN TURN, AS THOUGH THEY WERE CHILDREN, PRECIOUS CONFIDANTS, OLD FRIENDS AND MERRY COMPANIONS. THESE SENSITIVE LARGE ANIMALS CANNOT BE FOOLED AND IMMEDIATELY RECOGNIZE A WOMAN WHO LOVES THEM AND BELONGS TO THEIR WORLD, WITH WHOM THEY CAN HAVE A TRUE CONVERSATION WITHOUT WORDS, WITH WHOM THEY CAN SHARE A RECKLESS GALLOP AND A GENTLE CARESS. THEY RUMMAGE IN HER POCKETS, MUSS UP HER MOP OF BLOND HAIR, THRUST THEIR INTRUSIVE NOSES INTO HER CHEST, WINK AND TRUSTINGLY ABANDON THEMSELVES TO HER GENEROUS TOUCH.

OVER THE YEARS PHOTOGRAPHY HAS QUIETLY PLAYED ITS OWN ROLE IN THIS RELATIONSHIP, NOT AS AN INTRUDER, BUT RATHER AS A SUPPORT AND A MEANS OF ELEVATING THIS VERY CARNAL BOND AND SHARING IT WITH OTHER HORSE LOVERS.

GABRIELE HAS HAD TWO GREAT PASSIONS SINCE CHILDHOOD: HORSES AND PHOTOGRAPHY. HER MOTHER, WHO CAME FROM A FAMILY OF FARMERS AND BREEDERS THAT HAD OWNED HORSES FOR GENERATIONS, TRANSMITTED THE FIRST OF THESE. THE SECOND COMMENCED AT THE AGE OF 14, WHEN HER FATHER PRESENTED HER WITH HER FIRST CAMERA. HOWEVER, THE IDEA OF BECOMING A HORSE PHOTOGRAPHER CAME MUCH LATER. AS A YOUNGSTER, GABRIELE WANTED TO BE A JOURNALIST AND RELEGATE HORSES TO THE SPHERES OF LEISURE AND RELAXATION. SHE LEFT THE LITTLE CITY OF SPEYER, IN SOUTHWEST GERMANY, AND MOVED TO FRANKFURT AND THEN BERLIN. SHE STARTED WRITING FOR NEWSPAPERS AND WANT-

ED TO WORK IN TELEVISION AND MAKE A NAME FOR HERSELF, FREQUENTING THE NEWSROOMS, SOCIETY EVENINGS AND

VERNISSAGES. HOWEVER, HER TRUE VOCATION CONSTANTLY BECKONED AND TORMENTED HER. SHE WAS TOO INDEPENDENT

TO CONFORM TO THE MODELS OF THE TIME, TOO ENTHUSIASTIC TO LEARN TO STAY QUIET, AND TOO ADVENTUROUS TO RE-

MAIN SEATED AT A DESK. AND SO GABRIELE PACKED HER BAGS AND LEFT WITH HER CAMERA AROUND HER NECK, TRAVELING

THE WORLD INSTEAD OF DEDICATING HERSELF TO SOCIAL LIFE, EXCHANGING THE CORRIDORS OF AIRPORTS FOR THOSE OF

THE NEWSROOMS. OF COURSE, SHE MET HORSES EVERYWHERE HER CURIOSITY TOOK HER. AND RIDERS, WHO – LIKE HER –

THINK, SPEAK AND BREATHE HORSES. THE JOURNALIST DECIDED TO BEAR WITNESS TO THESE EQUESTRIAN CULTURES; THE

PASSIONATE WOMAN HOPED TO PAY TRIBUTE TO THEM; AND THE PHOTOGRAPHER DESIRED TO IMPOSE HER STYLE ON THIS

TASK. HOWEVER, FIRST IT WAS NECESSARY TO FIND IT.

AT THE BEGINNING OF THE 1980S, GABRIELE TRAVELED TO VARIOUS ARAB COUNTRIES TO PHOTOGRAPH THE FINEST HORS-

ES OF THE *HARAS* (STUDS). SHE, WITH HER INTIMATE KNOWLEDGE OF THE EUROPEAN BREEDS – THE ELEGANCE OF THE SPORT-

ING HORSES AND THE STRENGTH OF THE DRAFT HORSES – FELL UTTERLY AND DEFINITIVELY UNDER THE SPELL OF THE MAG-

NIFICENT "DRINKER OF THE WIND." THE SHOCK OF AN ENCOUNTER WITH A PUREBRED ARABIAN STALLION IN THE ENCHANT-

ED SETTING OF AN EGYPTIAN *HARAS* PROVED TO BE THE TURNING POINT OF HER ENTIRE CAREER. DURING HER VISIT TO THE

EL ZAHRAA STUD FARM, ON THE OUTSKIRTS OF CAIRO, AN EXCEPTIONAL HORSE SUDDENLY APPEARED, GALLOPING BEFORE

HER EYES WITH UNMATCHED GRACE AND BEAUTY. THE HANDSOME ECHNATON (FOR THIS WAS HIS NAME) CONQUERED THE

HORSEWOMAN WITH HIS CHARM, CAPTURING HER SENSE OF BEAUTY AND CHALLENGING HER TALENT AS A PHOTOGRAPHER.

GABRIELE FIXED AN APPOINTMENT AT THE *HARAS* TO ORGANIZE A PHOTO SHOOT THE VERY NEXT DAY. THE NOBLE ANIMAL

ONCE AGAIN DEMONSTRATED HIS LIGHTNESS AND FLUIDITY COMBINED WITH HIS DAZZLING ENERGY, WHILE THE YOUNG

WOMAN TRIED TO CAPTURE THE DISPLAY ON FILM TO BEST EFFECT. HOWEVER, HER EFFORTS WERE IN VAIN. WHEN SHE VIEWED

THE SHOTS THE FOLLOWING DAY, ALL HER CONVICTIONS FALTERED, FOR SHE SENSED THE CRUEL GAP BETWEEN THE MAGIC

AND ENCHANTMENT THAT SHE HAD TWICE EXPERIENCED WITH HER MODEL AND THE FLATNESS OF THE PRINTED IMAGES. FOL

LOWING THIS DISAPPOINTMENT AND HUMILIATION, GABRIELE TOOK A DECISION THAT WAS TO CHANGE THE COURSE OF HER

10   This is the essence of the Andalusian: gentle eyes, rounded forms, and a docile nature that allows it to accept such a controlling bit. Andalusia, the quintessential land of horsemen, is another exceptional source of inspiration for my photographs.

LIFE: FROM THAT TIME ON SHE WOULD TIRELESSLY PURSUE THE NOBILITY AND BEAUTY OF THE ARABIAN HORSE UNTIL MANAGING TO REPRESENT IT IN HER PHOTOGRAPHS.

FOUR YEARS AND HUNDREDS OF FILMS LATER, THE PHOTOGRAPHER DECIDED SHE HAD MADE SUFFICIENT PROGRESS TO ALLOW HER WORK TO BE PUBLISHED. THE RESULT WAS HER FIRST CALENDAR WITH HER 12 FINEST PHOTOGRAPHS OF ARABIAN HORSES. SHE ENTITLED IT FASCINATION, IN TRIBUTE TO HER MODELS AND THE SENTIMENT THAT THEY INSPIRE IN HER. IT WAS 1984, AND GABRIELE FOUNDED EDITIONS BOISELLE TO REPRESENT AND PROTECT THIS WORK IN FRANCE AND GERMANY, SUBSEQUENTLY EXTENDING ITS SCOPE TO THE ENTIRE WORLD. OVER 20 YEARS LATER, THE BOISELLE STYLE HAS CONQUERED THE HORSE-LOVING WORLD ON ALL CONTINENTS, ALTHOUGH THE PHOTOGRAPHER CONTINUES TO PURSUE HER DREAM OF PERFECTION. YOU NEED ONLY TO SEE ONE OF HER HORSE PORTRAITS TO BE STRUCK BY HER INIMITABLE STYLE, WITH ITS VERY SPECIAL POETRY THAT EXUDES PURE POWER AND CONQUERS YOU FOREVER. IT'S ENOUGH TO GLANCE AT THE COVER OF A MAGAZINE OR A CALENDAR TO AFFIRM WITHOUT HESITATION, "THAT'S BY BOISELLE." THIS ACHIEVEMENT – A "SIGNATURE" THAT DISTINGUISHES ONE'S WORK FROM THAT OF EVERYONE ELSE – IS EVERY PHOTOGRAPHER'S DREAM. GABRIELE ALWAYS SEEMS TO DOUBT AND QUESTION HERSELF, AWAITING ENCOURAGEMENT AND APPROVAL FOR HER WORK. THE SUCCESS OF HER PHOTOS AND THE ADMIRATION OF HER COLLEAGUES NEVER FAIL TO AMAZE HER. NONETHELESS, SHE CONTINUES TO FEEL FAR FROM HER GOAL, SET IN THE EARLY 1980S IN AN EGYPTIAN HARAS.

I'VE OFTEN DISAGREED WITH GABRIELE'S CLAIM THAT SHE CONVEYS BUT A PALE REFLECTION OF TRUE BEAUTY. INSTEAD, SHE ELEVATES IT AND CAPTURES IT IN A SURPRISINGLY POETIC MANNER. I'VE ACCOMPANIED HER ON COUNTLESS PHOTO SHOOTS, WHERE THE HORSE WAS HANDSOME, BUT NOT EXTRAORDINARY, THE SETTING FAR FROM PERFECT, THE WEATHER DULL.... GABRIELE PERUSES AND MEASURES THE LOCATION, OBSERVES THE HORSE, REFLECTS FOR A FEW MINUTES AND THEN RUMMAGES IN HER HUGE PHOTOGRAPHER'S BAG AND ISSUES ORDERS: THE HORSE MUST BE IN THAT POSITION, IN FRONT OF THAT BACKDROP, AT THAT TIME. AN IMAGE FORMS IN HER MIND'S EYE AND SHE NEVER CEASES TO PURSUE IT, TAKING HUNDREDS OF PHOTOGRAPHS AND RETURNING SEVERAL TIMES UNTIL DRIVING THE OWNERS ALMOST CRAZY, FOR THEY CAN'T MANAGE TO UNDERSTAND WHAT THIS MYSTERIOUS WOMAN IS SEEKING. THEY KNOW THAT THE END RESULTS WILL BE AS STRIK-

ING AS HER PREVIOUS PHOTOGRAPHS, BUT THEY RARELY UNDERSTAND THE METHOD AND THE WORK NECESSARY TO MAKE THOSE RESULTS POSSIBLE. IT'S ONLY WHEN THEY DISCOVER THE RESULT ON THEIR COMPUTER SCREENS THAT THEY SUDDENLY DROP THEIR DEFENSES AND FINALLY SEE WHAT THEIR HEARTS HAD LONG SUGGESTED ABOUT THEIR HORSES: THEIR INNER BEAUTY, GREAT STRENGTH, NOBILITY, SENSITIVITY AND GRACE. EVERYTHING'S THERE, IN PHOTOGRAPHS THAT IMMORTALIZE THE GLORY OF WHAT ARE NONETHELESS ORDINARY ANIMALS IN EVERYDAY LIFE. MANY PHOTOGRAPHS REQUIRE THE TRANSPORTATION OF THE HORSES TO OTHER SETTINGS, SUCH AS A BEACH. IN THE DEEP OF NIGHT A TEAM PREPARES THE MODELS, LOADS THEM, FENCES AND SECURES THE SPACE IN WHICH THEY WILL BE RELEASED AT FIRST LIGHT TO SHOOT THE PHOTOS. SEVERAL ASSISTANTS RIDE BEHIND TO DIRECT THE ENTHUSIASTIC GALLOPS OF AN ANIMAL OVERJOYED TO HAVE REDISCOVERED ITS FREEDOM. OTHERS CARRY LUNGE WHIPS TO TRY TO STOP IT, PLASTIC BAGS OR UMBRELLAS TO ATTRACT ITS ATTENTION, BRUSHES FOR QUICK TOUCHUPS BETWEEN SHOTS, AND SO ON. THE READER MAY PROTEST THAT ALL OF THIS IS ARTIFICIAL, BUT GABRIELE INSTEAD AIMS TO RESTORE THE HORSE'S NATURAL SPLENDOR IN A SETTING AS SIMILAR AS POSSIBLE TO ITS ORIGINAL FREE STATE, FAR FROM DARK STABLES, ENCLOSED RACECOURSES AND FENCED PADDOCKS. RELEASED IN A NATURAL SETTING, INEBRIATED BY THE SPACE, THE HORSE REDISCOVERS ITS JOIE DE VIVRE, WILD POWER AND FINEST EXPRESSIONS, AS TESTIFIED BY THE PHOTOGRAPHS.

GABRIELE'S WORK DOES NOT, HOWEVER, MERELY CONSIST OF THESE ORGANIZED SHOTS. I OFTEN SEE HER VERY SIMPLY ENJOYING THE PLEASURE OF CAPTURING THE IMAGES THAT PASS BEFORE HER EYES. SHE PLACES HERSELF AMONG THE HORSES IN A FIELD, ROLLING IN THE GRASS TO PLAY WITH FOALS THAT NIP HER CLOTHES AND RESPONDING TO STALLIONS THAT APPROACH TO PROVOKE HER. SHE WAITS, LETTING HER GAZE ROAM UNTIL HER LENS MANAGES TO CAPTURE THE HORSE IN A MOMENT OF TRUTH, WHEN IT SURRENDERS COMPLETELY, AS THOUGH IN THE PRESENCE OF ANOTHER OF ITS KIND. THIS MAY LAST HOURS, SOMETIMES IN TERRIBLE WEATHER CONDITIONS. GABRIELE SHIVERS IN THE ICELANDIC SNOW AND WIND, OR SWEATS BENEATH THE OPPRESSIVE MOROCCAN SUN, BUT HER EYES REMAIN GLUED TO THE CAMERA UNTIL SHE MANAGES TO CAPTURE AN EMOTION, CONTINUING AS LONG AS THE HORSE HAS SOMETHING TO CONVEY.

SOMETIMES, WHEN WE'RE IN THE CAR TRAVELING TO AN APPOINTMENT, SHE SUDDENLY PULLS OVER TO THE SIDE OF THE ROAD AND DASHES INTO THE FIELDS WITH HER CAMERA, FORGETTING THE TIME, HER OBLIGATIONS AND EVEN HER PHONE,

WHICH RINGS INCREASINGLY INSISTENTLY. THE REST OF THE WORLD SEEMS TO DISAPPEAR: GABRIELE HAS SEEN A HANDSOME NEW HORSE OR A DONKEY, WHOSE EARS SHE MUST STROKE. SHE PLAYS WITH THE CAMERA AND HER IMPROVISED MODELS, CATCHING HER SMART SUIT ON THE BUSHES, DIRTYING HER SHOES IN THE GRASS AND LETTING THE HORSES RUB THEMSELVES AGAINST HER COAT. THEN THE PLAYFUL GIRL RETURNS TO THE CAR, WITH PIECES OF CHEWED HAY IN HER HAIR, FORGETTING THE TWO HOURS SPENT AT THE HAIRDRESSER SO THAT SHE COULD ARRIVE AT HER APPOINTMENT LOOKING IMPECCABLE. SHE LAUGHS, FRUITLESSLY TRIES TO RESTORE A PRESENTABLE APPEARANCE, THEN TEARS OFF IN AN ATTEMPT TO MAKE UP FOR HER LATENESS. AFTER 25 YEARS SPENT PHOTOGRAPHING HORSES, THE READER MIGHT EXPECT HER EYES TO TIRE, HER CREATIVITY TO DRY UP AND HER ENTHUSIASM TO FLAG. HOWEVER, GABRIELE'S PASSION FOR PHOTOGRAPHY SEEMS TO BE INEXHAUSTIBLE. INDEED, SHE APPEARS TO LOSE SOME OF HER ENERGY AND FRESHNESS AFTER A FEW DAYS WITHOUT TAKING PHOTOGRAPHS, AND BECOMES BORED. SHE MISSES PHOTOGRAPHY BOTH PHYSICALLY AND MENTALLY, AND HAS TO LEAVE HER STUDIO AND HEAD FOR THE ROADS OR AIRPORTS IN SEARCH OF DESTINATIONS WITH DREAM HORSES AND NEW PICTURES. THIS IS HOW SHE FUELS HER IMAGINATION, SENSE OF BEAUTY AND THIRST FOR HARMONY. FEET ON THE GROUND, EYES GLUED ON A MANE STREAMING IN THE WIND OR A CARACOLING RUMP, SHE REDISCOVERS THE CONSTANTS OF HER LIFE.

HOWEVER, WITHOUT HORSES AND PHOTOGRAPHS, THIS FORCE OF NATURE DWINDLES AND GABRIELE BECOMES SICK, STOPS LAUGHING AND THEN WORKING… UNTIL SHE CAN'T DO ANYTHING. I HONESTLY THINK THAT SHE COULD DIE, SLOWLY BURNING HERSELF OUT. PERHAPS IT IS PRECISELY THIS WEAKNESS THAT GIVES SO MUCH POWER TO HER PHOTOS, THIS DEEPLY TOUCHING AND VITAL BOND WITH HORSES. VERY FEW PHOTOGRAPH ARE ABLE TO MAKE YOUR STOMACH CHURN OR CAUSE YOU TO BREAK OUT IN GOOSEFLESH, BUT GABRIELE'S IMAGES MANAGE TO DO SO, BECAUSE THEY CONVEY THE ESSENTIAL: BEAUTY BEYOND REALITY, PO-ETRY TO COMBAT BARBARISM, SPIRITUALITY TO ELEVATE THE EVERYDAY. THEY REMIND US OF THE REASON WHY OUR BOND WITH HORSES HAS ALWAYS BEEN SO STRONG SINCE THE DAWN OF TIME – OUR FASCINATION WITH THEIR WILD POWER, THE STRENGTH THAT THEY INFUSE IN US TO ALLOW US TO SURPASS OURSELVES, AND THE WISDOM THAT THEY TEACH US DAY AFTER DAY.

LIKE ALL REAL WORKS OF ART, THAT OF GABRIELE BOISELLE OPENS OUR EYES TO THE WORLD AND TO OURSELVES.

AGNÈS GALLETIER

grace and beauty

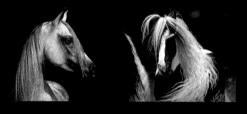

grace and beauty

TO MY EYES, THE GRACE AND BEAUTY OF THE HORSE ARE INSEPARABLE FROM THE PUREBRED ARABIAN, FOR NO OTH-

ER BREED HAS SUCH CHARISMA, DAZZLING ENERGY AND NATURAL ELEGANCE.

I STILL FEEL A SORT OF SHIVER WHEN I THINK OF MY FIRST ENCOUNTER, 25 YEARS AGO, WITH AN ARABIAN STALLION

CALLED ECHNATON AT THE EL ZAHRAA EGYPTIAN NATIONAL STUD.

I REMEMBER ARRIVING AT THE STUD FARM ABOARD AN ANCIENT YELLOW TAXI THAT WAS MIRACULOUSLY STILL IN

WORKING ORDER. WE TRAVELED ALONG A PALM-LINED AVENUE, WILTING IN THE SEARING SUMMER HEAT. IT MUST HAVE

BEEN MIDDAY WHEN WE FINALLY ARRIVED. THE BIRDS WERE SILENT, NOT EVEN A BREEZE RUSTLED THE LEAVES OF THE

TREES, AND NO SENSIBLE MAN WOULD HAVE VENTURED OUT UNDER THAT BLISTERING SUN. EVEN THE EARTH HAD BE-

COME DUST, AND WE WERE ALONE, LOST IN AN OCEAN OF BLINDING LIGHT.

HOWEVER, THE SILENCE AND STILLNESS WERE SUDDENLY BROKEN BY A WHIRL OF DUST HURTLING TOWARD US. IN ITS

MIDST I COULD MAKE OUT THE FANTASTIC AND DREAMLIKE IMAGE OF A GRAY STALLION, FLOATING RATHER THAN GAL-

LOPING AND RAISING CLOUDS OF DUST WITH HIS HOOVES AT EACH STRIDE. HIS MOVEMENTS HAD A DANCER'S GRACE AND

A LIGHTNESS AND FLUIDITY THAT SEEMED UNEARTHLY IN SUCH A LARGE ANIMAL. HIS EXPRESSION, CARRIAGE AND HEAD

EMANATED A PRINCELY DIGNITY. OPEN-MOUTHED AND WIDE-EYED, I WAS HYPNOTIZED BY THE VISION.

FROM THE DAY THAT I FIRST SAW HIM ECHNATON IMPRESSED AN IMAGE OF ABSOLUTE, UNCHANGEABLE AND ALMOST

UNREAL BEAUTY ON ME. THAT EMOTION AND VIBRANT MEMORY HAVE UNDOUBTEDLY INFLUENCED THE REST OF MY LIFE

AND MY WORK.

THE FOLLOWING MORNING I RETURNED WITH MY CAMERA TO TRY TO CAPTURE EVEN A FRAGMENT OF THAT MAGIC. HOWEVER, THE RESULTS WERE DISASTROUS AND EXTREMELY DISAPPOINTING. I CRIED WITH DISAPPOINTMENT OVER THE PHOTOGRAPHS, FOR THERE WAS ABSOLUTELY NO RELATION BETWEEN MY ASTONISHING EXPERIENCE AND THE PAUCITY AND FLATNESS OF WHAT I HAD BEFORE MY EYES. IT WAS IN THAT PRECISE MOMENT THAT MY LIFETIME QUEST AS A PHOTOGRAPHER COMMENCED. MY AIM WAS TO IMMORTALIZE THE EMOTION AROUSED BY CLOSE CONTACT WITH HORSES AND TO SHARE THIS FLEETING, VOLATILE AND ALMOST ABSTRACT VISION AND MYSTERIOUS EXPERIENCE WITH THOSE WHO WOULD LATER VIEW MY WORK FROM OUTSIDE ITS CONTEXT.

ECHNATON'S LESSON STILL FORMS THE BASIS FOR MY WORK TODAY AND I FOLLOW THE SAME PROCEDURE EACH TIME THAT I PREPARE A SHOT: FIRST I "LISTEN" TO MY SENSATIONS IN THE PRESENCE OF THE HORSE, ALLOWING MYSELF TIME TO BE IMBUED WITH ITS BEAUTY, CHARISMA AND PERSONALITY. THEN I CLOSE MY EYES AND IMAGINE A PHOTOGRAPH CAPABLE OF REPLICATING THE SAME SENSATION, THE STILL IMAGE THAT WILL CONVEY THE EMOTION, GRACE OF MOVEMENT AND INTENSITY OF EXPRESSION. WHEN I REOPEN MY EYES, I KNOW WHAT I WANT AND THUS TRY TO DIRECT THE WORK SESSION TOWARD THAT SPECIFIC GOAL.

WHILE IT IS TRUE THAT I ADAPT MYSELF TO MY MODEL, SEEKING ITS MOST BEAUTIFUL AND GRACEFUL ASPECTS,

17   Frédéric Pignon's show horse, Templado, seems very aware of his fine looks.

18 and 19   The grace of the Andalusian is matched only by its strength. The capriole is one of the most difficult haute-école airs: the horse must leap into the air and kick out its hind legs. This horse is ridden by one of the extraordinary riders and trainers of the Royal Andalusian School of Equestrian Art of Jerez.

grace and beauty

grace and beauty

MY QUEST DOES NOT STOP THERE. EACH TIME THAT I TAKE PHOTO-GRAPHS, I TRY TO CAPTURE A FRAGMENT OF THE GRACE AND BEAUTY OF HORSES IN THEIR ENTIRETY. A SURPRISING UNIQUENESS IS REFLECTED IN EACH OF THEM, WITH A PARTICULAR TINGE, LIKE THE CHANGING FACETS OF THE SAME UNIVERSE.

ALL HORSES ARE BEAUTIFUL AND I OFTEN PULL OVER TO THE SIDE OF THE ROAD AND CLIMB THE FENCE OF THEIR ENCLOSURE TO PHOTOGRAPH THEM. I'M NOT TALKING ABOUT GRAND PRIX ATHLETES, THE RACEHORSES OF SOME EMIR, OR THE PERSONAL STABLE OF A RICH OWNER, BUT HORS-ES GRAZING PEACEFULLY IN THEIR FIELD, WHO CURIOUSLY WATCH ME AR-RIVE WITH ALL MY EQUIPMENT. EVEN THE SO-CALLED "HEAVY" HORSES CAN EXPRESS GRACE, NOT ALWAYS IN THEIR MOVEMENTS, BUT OFTEN IN THEIR EXPRESSION. I NEVER CEASE TO BE SURPRISED BY THEIR GREAT DIG-NITY, THE WISDOM OF THEIR GAZE AND THE STYLIZED NATURE OF THEIR SLOW MOVEMENTS.

THE GRACE OF AN ANDALUSIAN, DERIVED FROM ITS HARMONIOUS LINES AND NOBILITY, IS NOT THE SAME AS THAT OF A THOROUGHBRED, WHICH IS AN INTRIGUING BLEND OF ELEGANCE AND LIVELINESS. THE LEAN, LONG-LIMBED AKHAL-TEKE OF THE DESERT IS THE EXACT OPPOSITE OF THE MASSIVE AND SOLID FRIESIAN. EVEN A SHETLAND PONY IS BEAU-

TIFUL AND NOT SIMPLY PRETTY, AND THIS CONCENTRATE OF HORSE BE-COMES AN UNBEATABLE MODEL IF ALLOWED TO EXPRESS ITS VITALITY AND IMMENSE FORCE AND REVEAL ITS STRONG CHARACTER.

EVERYTHING ABOUT THE HORSE IS BEAUTIFUL: THE DELICATE FORM OF ITS SOFT NOSTRILS, THE NOBLE PROFILE OF ITS HEAD, ITS FINELY CHIS-ELED EARS, ITS SILKY MANE, ITS ARCHED NECK, ITS POWERFUL CHEST, ITS ROUNDED FLESHY RUMP AND ITS SLENDER LEGS. EACH STEP SEEMS STUD-IED, EACH MOVEMENT EXUDES GRACE AND EACH EXPRESSION IS VIBRANT. THE SIMPLE GESTURE OF TURNING ITS HEAD OR EXTENDING ITS NECK TO APPROACH A STRANGER WARILY WITH ITS NOSE, REVEALS THE DELICACY OF THIS EXCEPTIONAL ANIMAL AND THE HARMONY OF ITS UNIVERSE. IN-DEED, THE WORLD OF THE HORSE APPEARS TOTALLY REMOVED FROM VUL-GARITY, BANALITY AND MEDIOCRITY.

HORSES THEMSELVES SEEM TO THINK THAT BEAUTY ALONE ISN'T ENOUGH AND DO THEIR BEST TO SHOW OFF, TRYING TO ASTOUND US AND LEAVE US LOST FOR WORDS. ALL IT TAKES IS A FEW SPECTATORS OR A GROUP OF ADMIRERS AND OUR ANGEL CHANGES INTO A DANDY. HE RAISES HIS NOSE, ROLLS HIS EYES, DILATES HIS NOSTRILS, FLEXES HIS NECK, SWISHES HIS TAIL LIKE A FLAG, ALTERS AND EXAGGERATES HIS GAIT, SEEMING TO BEAT THE AIR WITH HIS HOOVES, BUT IN A PERFECTLY CON-

TROLLED MANNER. HE PROUDLY PAWS THE GROUND, KICKS AND REARS, STRUTTING BEFORE OUR ADMIRING EYES. HE IS WELL AWARE THAT ALL THE ATTENTION IS ON HIM AND MISCHIEVOUSLY PLAYS FOR OUR PLEASURE, AS THOUGH HE KNOWS THAT WE LIKE NOTHING BETTER. AFTER A FEW MINUTES OF THE SPECTACLE, CERTAIN OF HAVING SATISFIED HIS COURT OF ADMIRERS, HE ONCE AGAIN BECOMES THE WELL-BALANCED AND HAUGHTY LORD AND RETURNS TO THE STABLE WITH MAJESTIC CALM.

THE HORSE'S BEAUTY SEEMS TO HAVE A RARE AND DISCONCERTINGLY UNIVERSAL APPEAL. EVEN THE LEAST IMPORTANT NAG CAUSES EXCLAMATIONS OF WONDER AS IT CROSSES THE STREETS OF A VILLAGE: "A HORSE, A HORSE! COME AND SEE HIM! HE'S LOVELY!" SHOUT CHILDREN WORLDWIDE, AS THEY RUN TO PAT HIM. EVERYONE IS DRAWN TO THAT FLEETING VISION THAT IMMEDIATELY DEPARTS TOWARD ITS OWN FANTASY WORLD, AS THOUGH A FIGMENT OF THE IMAGINATION. OLD PEOPLE SMILE TENDERLY AND FIND THEMSELVES BACK IN THEIR YOUTH ACCOMPANIED BY THE SOUND OF HOOVES RINGING OUT ON THE FLAGSTONES, WHILE OTHERS WATCH FROM A DISTANCE, THEIR EYES BETRAYING THE MIXTURE OF FASCINATION AND FEAR THAT HORSES AROUSE IN THOSE WHO DON'T KNOW THEM.

THIS ANIMAL CONVEYS MAGIC, RESTORES DREAMS AND BESTOWS MARVELS: A PEGASUS WHO LENDS US HIS WINGS FOR A WHILE, BRINGING US CLOSER TO HEAVEN AND ALLOWING US TO FORGET THE HARSH LAWS OF REALITY FOR A MOMENT. MAN IS CLOSER TO GOD WHEN MOUNTED ON A HORSE, FOR HE IS ELEVATED IN THE NOBLEST SENSE OF THE WORD.

INDEED, FOR HORSE LOVERS THE MOST MOVING ASPECT OF THE HORSE – BESIDES ITS PHYSICAL GRACE AND NOBLE GAIT – IS UNDOUBTEDLY ITS SPLENDID SPIRIT. THIS ANIMAL TOUCHES OUR INNERMOST SOUL, SATISFIES OUR CRAVING FOR BEAUTY AND QUENCHES OUR THIRST FOR THE ABSOLUTE. IT'S AS THOUGH ITS PRESENCE AND NEARNESS GIVE US THE STRENGTH TO DEAL WITH THE TRIALS OF DAILY LIFE, THE SERIES OF COMPROMISES AND MEAN ACTS, AND THE RESTRICTIONS CONSTANTLY IMPOSED ON US. ITS BEAUTY SOOTHES OUR TROUBLES, CLEANSES OUR SOULS AND INVIGORATES US, AND THIS IS PRECISELY THE STATE OF THE RIDER WHEN HE LEAVES THE STABLES, PURIFIED AND FULL OF RESOURCES AND NEW ENERGY. BEAUTY HAS PERFORMED ITS TASK, AS THOUGH IT HAD DECIDED TO AID US IN THE SHAPE OF THE HORSE'S HARMONIOUS BODY AND PURE SPIRIT.

THIS IS UNDOUBTEDLY ALSO THE REASON WHY ART OWES SO MUCH TO THE HORSE. THIS HANDSOME ANIMAL HAS BEEN DEPICTED IN ALL IMAGINABLE FORMS BY ALL CIVILIZATIONS AND IN ALL AGES, FROM THE

20   A Friesian stallion photographed on the shores of an American lake. Despite being surrounded by the highways leading to Los Angeles, the horse manages to make us forget all about them: all we see is his majestic beauty.

22-23   The Lusitano stallion Ibanil in the early morning light, as he emerges from the ocean on an Andalusian beach.

25   The grace and gentleness of an Arabian bear witness to this horse's great elegance, which is accompanied by an unusual sensitivity.

FIRST PREHISTORIC ROCK PAINTINGS TO ROMAN STATUES, CHINESE PORCELAIN AND DELACROIX'S SKETCHES. MOST OF THE STATUES IN CITIES THROUGHOUT THE WORLD ARE EQUESTRIAN. INDEED, THE PRESENCE OF A MAN – HOWEVER CELEBRATED – WOULD NOT BE THE SAME WITHOUT HIS STEED. TODAY'S ARTISTS ARE STILL FASCINATED BY HORSES AND THE FORCE WITH WHICH THEY IMBUE ANY WORK, BUT ALSO BY THE DIFFICULTY AND GREAT CHALLENGE OF TRYING TO REPRODUCE THEIR NATURAL HARMONY.

MAN, WHO WISHES TO TAKE POSSESSION OF EVERYTHING, HAS THUS TRIED – AND CONTINUES TO TRY – TO MAKE THE HORSE'S GRACE HIS OWN AND BECOME ITS SECOND CREATOR. THE FOREMOST EXAMPLE OF THIS ATTEMPT IS TO BE FOUND IN DRESSAGE, OR HAUTE ÉCOLE. THE NAME COULD LEAD THE NOVICE TO BELIEVE THAT IT TRAINS THE HORSE TO DEVELOP ITS GRACE YET FURTHER, REFINING ITS MOVEMENTS AND ENLIVENING ITS CARRIAGE, BUT THE PURPOSE OF MANY OF THE EXERCISES IS ACTUALLY TO MAKE IT DO WHAT IT DOES NATURALLY!

THUS THE *PIAFFES* (A CADENCED TROT), *PASSAGES* AND FABULOUS EXTENSIONS THAT IT USES EXCLUSIVELY FOR PURPOSES OF INTIMIDATION OR SEDUCTION HAVE BEEN CODIFIED BY MAN, ALONG WITH ITS GAITS, FOR PERFORMANCE ON DEMAND. THE APPROPRIATION IS THUS COM-

grace and beauty

PLETE: THE RIDER NOT ONLY BENEFITS FROM THE HORSE'S NATURAL ELE-GANCE, BUT ALSO TAKES POSSESSION OF THE TOOLS OF SEDUCTION THAT IT RESERVES FOR ITS INTIMATE ACQUAINTANCES.

NO OTHER ANIMAL IS THE FOCUS OF SO MUCH ATTENTION AND SUCH AN EXTENSIVE CULTURE IN TERMS OF GROOMING AND EMBELLISHMENT. EVEN DOGS, UPON WHICH WE LAVISH MUCH AFFECTION, ARE NEVER AS ELABORATELY ADORNED, GROOMED, DRESSED AND ACCESSORIZED AS HORSES. WE HAVE CREATED TRUE JEWELS, ENCRUSTED WITH PEARLS AND PRECIOUS STONES FOR DISPLAY ON THEIR HARNESSES; STITCHED GOLD THREAD SADDLE CLOTHS; AND FASHIONED BITS THAT ARE MASTERPIECES OF THE GOLDSMITH'S ART. IN MANY PARTS OF THE WORLD THE CRAFTS AS-SOCIATED WITH HORSES ARE AMONG THE MOST COMPLEX AND LUXURI-OUS, AND CERTAIN SOUKS HAVE ENTIRE STREETS OF SADDLERS WHOSE PAINSTAKING WORK DRAWS RIDERS FROM ALL OVER THE COUNTRY. THE FRENCH SADDLER HERMÈS OFFERS MADE-TO-MEASURE TACK FOR HORSES, WHILE THE ENGLISH VIE WITH EACH OTHER IN TERMS OF INGENIOUSNESS AND TALENT IN THE PRODUCTION OF THE SOFTEST LEATHER IN THE WORLD. THE PRINCIPLE BEHIND THESE LUXURIOUS ACCESSORIES IS NOT SIMPLY COMFORT, BUT ALSO BEAUTY, AS THOUGH NOTHING WERE TOO BEAUTIFUL FOR HORSES. IN SOME COUNTRIES, SUCH AS INDIA, MAKEUP IS APPLIED TO HORSES AND THEIR MANES DYED WITH HENNA, WHILE THE AMERICAN INDIANS USED TO DRAW HANDS AND CIRCLES ON THEIR HORS-ES' BODIES AND THE BERBER WOMEN MADE BEADED NECKLACES FOR THEM.

IN THE WEST WE PLAIT THEIR MANES, TRIM HAIR THAT WE CONSIDER UNSIGHTLY (INSIDE THEIR EARS OR BENEATH THEIR HEADS) AND CLIP THEIR COATS IN VARIOUS PATTERNS, EACH OF WHICH HAS A SPECIAL NAME. SAD-DLECLOTHS, BOOTS, HALTERS AND HEAD-COLLARS IN ASSORTED COLORS, SILK BRUSHES AND BLANKETS EMBROIDERED WITH THE HORSE'S NAME: RID-ERS OFTEN SPEND MORE TIME ADORNING THEIR HORSES THAN RIDING THEM!

WHY IS THIS? THE REASONS INCLUDE PLEASURE, PRIDE AND THE WISH TO PAY TRIBUTE TO THE HORSE, ENHANCE ITS BEAUTY AND UNDOUBTEDLY TO APPROPRIATE IT. HOWEVER, IT DOESN'T MATTER: ALTHOUGH HORSES DON'T NEED THIS KIND OF ATTENTION, THEY NONETHELESS SEEM TO ENJOY IT, PLAYING ALONG WITH US AND WISELY ACCEPTING OUR VIBRANT TRIBUTE AND THIRST FOR PERFECTION. THEY LET THEMSELVES BE EMBELLISHED LIKE STARS, WITH MAKEUP ARTISTS AND HAIRDRESSERS BUSTLING AROUND THEM, AND FALL ASLEEP, LULLED BY THE ATTENTION.

HOWEVER, WHATEVER WE MAY DO, THE HORSE'S BEAUTY IS NOT OUR CREATION, FOR IT STRETCHES BACK OVER THOUSANDS OF YEARS, SPANS THE CONTINENTS AND MOCKS AT CULTURES AND FASHIONS. THE HORSE'S BEAUTY IS ABSOLUTE, UNADORNED AND COMPLETE. IT'S ETERNAL, AND AF-TER MANY YEARS – A QUARTER OF A CENTURY – SPENT FOLLOWING THIS AN-IMAL TO PHOTOGRAPH IT, I'M WELL AWARE THAT I STILL CAN'T CAPTURE ITS ESSENCE. SOMETIMES I APPROACH THIS GOAL, WITH THE IMPRESSION OF ALMOST HAVING ACHIEVED IT, BUT I ONLY NEED TO LOOK AT A HORSE AGAIN FOR MY ILLUSIONS TO DISAPPEAR, FOR I CAN SEE THAT THE IMAGE FOR WHICH I STRIVE CAN NEVER BE MORE THAN A MORE OR LESS FAITHFUL REFLECTION.

26-27　The beauty of the Friesian is not that of an Arabian prince, but that of an incredibly powerful armored fighter, which some people even find intimidating.
This ebony colossus combines the splendor of a luxuriant mane, rippling in the wind, with a high-stepping action worthy of a military parade.

grace and beauty

29 Ansata Nil Pacha was one of my most handsome models and an unending source of inspiration. Everything about him is beautiful: his perfect conformation, his naturally elegant movements and, above all, his inner power and the aura that he emanates.

30 and 31 Thoroughbreds "revealed" my job of photographer to me, fueling – and continuing to fuel – my continuous quest to improve my photographs. They are very photogenic, but nonetheless always leave me feeling frustrated, with the sorry sensation of never being able to convey their full beauty on film.

grace and beauty

32-33 A cloud of mane surrounds this handsome Haflinger stallion on the alert. The poetry expressed by a free horse in a natural setting is as touching as that of the finest animal kept in the smartest stables.

34-35   This galloping purebred Arabian resemble a dreamlike creature racing through our imagination, with its streaming tail, proudly held head and hooves that never seem to touch the ground.

36 and 37   The Egyptian *haras* opened the doors and the oriental charm of their stables to me, allowing me to discover horses graceful beyond my wildest dreams. True to its legend, the purebred Egyptian Arabian is undoubtedly one of the most handsome horses in the world.

38-39 This Friesian stallion exudes wild beauty, pride and nobility. This breed is the most admired and coveted by all young horsewomen, who dream of riding this incredibly powerful animal, which is far stronger than any other sporting horse.

grace and beauty

40 and 40-41   Anton is an uncommon horse: not only
is he surprisingly handsome, but he also dazes his admirers with
his personality, gentleness and dignity. I could spend my whole
life watching him, but I make do with simply spending hours
photographing him from all angles. He knows and poses for me,
although he always remains himself. I have the impression of
looking at a wise old man, with such a pure soul as to seem eternal
and timeless.

42 and 43 These hairy and mischievous little Gypsy Vanners reveal their origins as Irish gypsy horses, accustomed to great open spaces, traveling, and camps far away from quiet and orderly stables.

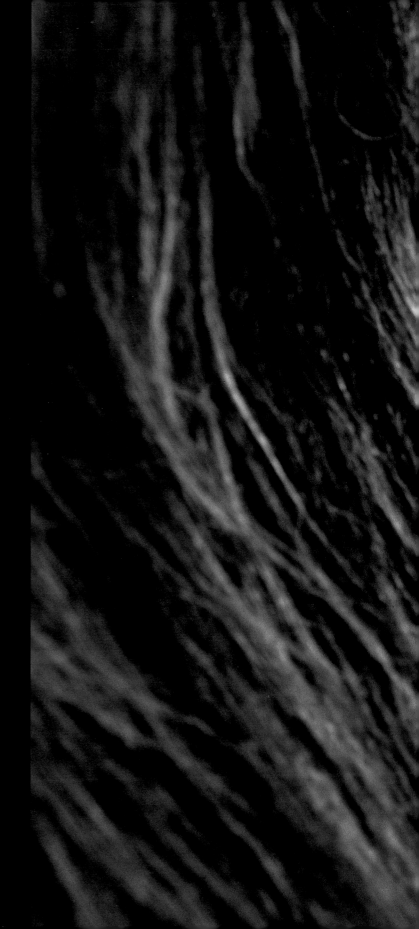

grace and beauty

44-45   I can always see something beautiful in all horses, whether they are large or small, thoroughbreds or ponies, not to mention heavy horses. This little shaggy-maned Icelandic pony, buffeted by the wind of its native island, moved me with its gentle and wise expression that nonetheless expressed its underlying freedom as a horse of the great open spaces.

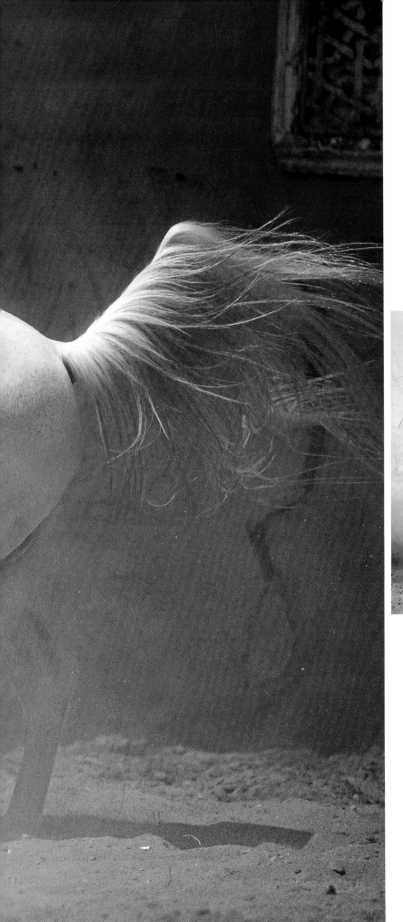

46-47 and 47 Pure lines, shapely curves and a soft silken coat gleaming in the sun: these purebred Arabians seem to float, flying rather than galloping. Their beauty is universal and eternal and it is to pay tribute to them that I have been taking photographs for over 25 years.

48-49 This purebred Spanish horse expresses all the power and gentleness of his breed, like a statue on a sand base. He brings to mind the rounded forms of ancient Chinese statues.

50 and 51   The El Zahraa Egyptian National Stud is home to horses as handsome as gods and as light as angels. The curve of the ocher-colored arches emphasizes the graceful lines of the necks of the purebred Arabians. This *haras* is one of the places that has fired my dreams and I have experienced the strongest emotions of my life between its walls, triggered by the boundless beauty of its inhabitants.

52-53   A body weighing over 1100 lbs (500 kg), which bounces like a ball and tenses like a bow, remaining suspended in flight with unnerving naturalness and self-assurance, defying the laws of gravity.

54-55 The Bedouins of North Africa have always paid tribute to the beauty of their horses by adorning them with jewelry, such as this necklace of blue beads. In the past this Arabian mare would have foaled beneath the tent, in the presence of the whole family, and the foal would have been raised among the children, who would have been its playmates.

56-57 The fire of an Arabian contrasts with the icy snow. These horses' thin skin and short coat, even during winter, seldom allows them to tolerate very cold temperatures.

58-59   A Haflinger stallion takes advantage of his momentary freedom on the shores of the North Sea, far from his original habitat in the Tyrolean Alps. This pony has inherited the qualities of his ancestors: the sturdiness of the medium-weight Austrian horses and the liveliness of Arabians.

60   A magical moment with a Friesian stallion who seems as though he wants to play with me. Despite the wind blowing in from the sea and the great expanse of sand around him, he is calm, peaceful and curious as to what he might do with this strange photographer.

61   It's six o'clock in the morning in Andalusia and a team of six people (not shown) is escorting this Lusitano released on the beach. Two are mounted to guide him, while the others are unrolling long, wide white tape to mark off a safety area. It's not always easy to release a horse in order to bring out its beauty.

62-63   Is it Poseidon emerging from the waters or a Friesian stallion enjoying a refreshing bath?

64-65   I traveled all the way to South Africa to photograph purebred Arabians. However, what I found more than recompensed the journey: radiantly beautiful horses and breathtakingly colorful landscapes.

66-67 *and* 67   Smudo is an exceptional Haflinger stallion, bred in Germany, where he has won all the possible shows for his breed. His generous rounded forms, mane and histrionic personality have won him many admirers.

68-69   Fluidity, grace, gentleness and strength, power and fragility: one's gaze is irresistibly attracted by the movement of this Haflinger's mane and you can almost hear the rhythm of his galloping hooves on the ground.

70-71   A Friesian galloping across the German countryside covered with spring dandelions.

72-73   I traveled to the South of France to photograph Templado. Much to my surprise, the weather was terrible. I was desperate, because I was unable to photograph this star of equestrian shows, who possesses an aura that seems to strike everyone who encounters him. However, we went outside with the camera and the horse despite the rain and gray skies. And the magic came too, defying the rain.

power and energy

power and energy

AS SOON AS YOU ENTER THE LOOSE BOX AND FASTEN HIS HALTER, YOUR HORSE STARTS FIDGETING. HE KNOWS THAT

AFTER HOURS OF WAITING, SEGREGATED IN THAT CONFINED SPACE, HE'LL FINALLY BE ABLE TO EXPRESS HIS TRUE SELF, THAT

OF AN ANIMAL BORN TO RUN AND BE FREE, AN ANIMAL OF THE GREAT OPEN SPACES. HE RESTLESSLY LEAVES THE LOOSE

BOX HEADING FOR THE PADDOCK, READY TO LEAP FORWARD, WARMING UP WITH LITTLE STRIDES BEFORE LETTING HIMSELF

GO COMPLETELY. ONCE YOU'RE THERE, MAKE SURE YOU RELEASE HIM WITHOUT DELAY, UNCLIPPING THE ROPE FROM THE

HALTER, BEFORE HE TEARS IT OUT OF YOUR HAND. HE CAN'T WAIT ANY LONGER; HIS PENT-UP ENERGY ESCAPES LIKE A RIV-

ER BURSTING ITS BANKS. ONCE A HORSE FINDS A WAY OUT, THE TUMULTUOUS WATERS OVERFLOW UNCONTROLLABLY,

READY TO DEVASTATE EVERYTHING IN THEIR PATH. THE RAGING RIVER CHURNS AND EXPRESSES ITSELF IN WAVES OF UN-

CONSTRAINED GALLOPING, KICKING, BUCKING, REARING, TURNING AND SWAYING, WITH MANE, TAIL AND HOOVES FLYING

IN ALL DIRECTIONS. HIS SURPLUS ENERGY, PENT UP FOR TOO LONG, EXPLODES LIKE A TIME BOMB.

IT IS UNDOUBTEDLY IN SUCH MOMENTS THAT HORSES APPEAR AT THEIR MOST HANDSOME AND IMPRESSIVE TO US. THE

PHOTOGRAPHS TAKEN DURING THE FIRST FEW MINUTES OF THIS DISPLAY CLEARLY REVEAL THEIR GREAT ENERGY AND

STRENGTH.

THOSE WHO ARE NOT FAMILIAR WITH HORSES ARE OFTEN FRIGHTENED BY THESE STRIKING DEMONSTRATIONS, IMAGIN-

ING THEMSELVES ON THE ANIMAL'S BACK IN AN INFERNAL RODEO. THEY WITNESS THE SCENE AS THOUGH IT WERE PROOF

OF THE WILD NATURE, AND THUS VIOLENCE, OF THE HORSE. HOWEVER, THOSE CLOSELY ACQUAINTED WITH THE ANIMAL

ARE TOUCHED TO SEE HIM RELEASING HIS NATURAL ENERGY, WHICH THEY KNOW IS PERFECTLY HEALTHY AND MORE RA-

TIONAL THAN IT APPEARS. THEY ENCOURAGE HIM IF HIS DISPLAYS ARE LIMPER THAN USUAL, OR TRY TO CALM HIM IF THEY

THINK HE'S OVERDOING IT AND IN DANGER OF HURTING HIMSELF, BUT THEY USUALLY SMILE AND ADMIRE THEIR COMPAN-

ION WITH A KNOWING GAZE.

LIKE A CHILD AFTER SCHOOL OR A PUPPY UNLEASHED, THE HORSE SURRENDERS TO PLEASURE AND PLAY, WITHOUT ANY

SIGNS OF AGGRESSIVENESS. HE INVENTS REASONS TO GO EVEN FASTER, PRETENDING TO KICK OUT AT THE ONLOOKER. AS

HE PLAYS, HE SEEMS TO REJOICE IN THE FREEDOM OF HIS MOVEMENT, BODY AND SPIRIT. AFTER HAVING ENJOYED THE

SIGHT OF THE HORSE PLAYING FOR A FEW MINUTES, HIS RIDER OR GROOM KNOWS THAT HE IS ONCE AGAIN READY TO LIS-

TEN TO REASON, PAY ATTENTION AND CONCENTRATE. THE FLOW OF THE RIVER HAS RESUMED ITS TRANQUIL PACE.

ONE OF THE GREATEST JOYS FOR A RIDER IS TO FEEL ALL THIS FANTASTIC ENERGY EXPRESSED BENEATH HIM AND WITH

HIM. OUR ARMS, LEGS AND ENTIRE BODIES FEEL THE HORSE RELEASING HIS POWER AND EXPRESSING HIS STRENGTH TO EAT

UP THE GROUND UNDER HIS HOOVES, JUMP A DITCH AS THOUGH IT WERE A CHASM AND TAKE OFF INTO INFINITE SPACE

AND THE UNKNOWN, FOR THE DESTINATION BECOMES IRRELEVANT. IT'S LIKE RIDING A CLOUD DURING A STORM, GLIDING

ON A TIDAL WAVE OR FEELING A VOLCANO RUMBLE BENEATH YOUR FEET. TIME NO LONGER EXISTS, SPACE HAS NO BOUND-

ARIES AND THE UNIVERSE HAS NO SECRETS. BY BECOMING A RIDER, VULNERABLE AND LIMITED MAN IS ADMITTED TO THE

MYSTERIES OF CREATION AND THE TELLURIAN ENERGY THAT UNITES HEAVEN AND EARTH.

AND AS WE GALLOP LIKE THE WIND, EYES STREAMING UNTIL THE HORIZON BECOMES A BLUR, HEART BEATING TO THE

RHYTHM OF THIS INFERNAL PACE, WE WISH THAT IT WOULD LAST FOREVER AND WANT TO CRY OUT WITH HAPPINESS, JOY

AND EXCITEMENT. ONLY OUR BRAIN BRINGS US BACK TO REALITY FOR A MOMENT, FOR IF WE SHOULD FALL, DEATH COULD

CLAIM OUR DISJOINTED BODIES. BUT WHO CARES? I'M READY TO GO ALL THE WAY TO HELL IF IT'S ON THE BACK OF MY

HORSE, GALLOPING FLAT OUT.

75   A herd of horses in Iceland.

76 left   Haflingers galloping.

76 center   A young Lusitano.

76 right   Haflingers race over the powdery snow.

78   The Portuguese stallion Ibanil gallops along a beach between Jerez and Cadiz.

power and energy

power and energy

THE HORSE INSTILLS IMMENSE STRENGTH IN MAN, ALLOWING HIM TO MULTIPLY HIS ENERGY, SPEED AND STAMINA TENFOLD, AND ALLOWING HIM TO EXPERIENCE A POWER AND A SENSATION OF HAVING GONE BEYOND HIS LIMITS UNKNOWN TO NON-RIDERS. THIS FEELING – WHICH WE ARE STILL ABLE TO PERCEIVE IN THE AGE OF AIR TRAVEL, CARS AND SUPER-POWERFUL ENGINES – MUST HAVE BEEN EVEN STRONGER WHEN THE ONLY OTHER DRIVING FORCE KNOWN TO MAN WAS THE STEADY PACE OF THE OX.

THE ENERGY THAT THE HORSE HAS GIVEN US HAS LEFT ITS MARK ON OUR SPIRIT AND OUR CULTURE, AND INDEED THE POWER OF MECHANICAL ENGINES IS STILL EXPRESSED IN TERMS OF HORSEPOWER TODAY, IN A FINAL TOKEN OF GRATITUDE OR TRIBUTE TO THESE ANIMALS THAT HAVE PUT THEMSELVES AT THE SERVICE OF HUMANKIND FOR THOUSANDS OF YEARS. WITHOUT THE HORSE TO DRAW PLOWS AND CARRIAGES, THRESH GRAIN, TOW BARGES, TRANSPORT MATERIALS OR FORM CAVALRY REGIMENTS, CIVILIZATION WOULD NEVER HAVE DEVELOPED AT THE SAME RATE. THE ENTIRE HISTORY OF THE WORLD TOOK A DIFFERENT COURSE AROUND 4000 YEARS AGO, WHEN MAN STARTED TO CONTROL AND RIDE THE HORSE. AT FIRST THE EQUESTRIAN REVOLUTION WAS TERRITORIAL AND TOOK THE FORM OF THE GREAT INVASIONS BY POPULATIONS OF GREAT RIDERS – HUNS, MONGOLS, MOORS – WHO CONQUERED LANDS STRETCHING FROM SOUTHERN EUROPE TO THE GREAT WALL OF CHINA MOUNTED ON THEIR BERBER AND ARABIAN STEEDS.

IN ADDITION TO THIS MILITARY STRENGTH, THE HORSE ALSO GAVE GREAT IMPETUS BOTH TRADE AND ALSO TO THE EARLY INDUSTRIAL AGE. IN 18TH-CENTURY MANCHESTER OVER 10,000 SHIRES, THE LARGEST DRAFT HORSES IN THE WORLD, WORKED AT THE DOCKS, LOADING AND UNLOADING THE VESSELS AROUND THE CLOCK. MILLIONS OF HORSES WORKED IN THE TOWNS AND CITIES, ON THE ROADS AND EVEN IN THE MINES, DRAWING THE WAGONS. WHOLE YEARS WOULD PASS WITHOUT THEM SEEING THE DAYLIGHT. UNTIL THE 1950S, WHEN TRACTORS REPLACED HORSES, EACH FARM HAD AT LEAST ONE OF THESE WORKERS THAT SERVED AS A TRUE ALL-ROUND ANIMAL FOR THE WHOLE FAMILY.

IF WE CONSIDER THE HUNDREDS OF MILLIONS OF HORSES THAT HAVE SERVED MAN OVER THE YEARS, DEDICATING THEIR ENERGY, INTELLIGENCE AND HEARTS TO US, WE REALLY DO HAVE GOOD REASON TO PAY TRIBUTE TO THESE ANIMALS AND OFFER THEM OUR MOST HEARTFELT THANKS.

THE POWER AND MARVELOUS ENERGY OF THE HORSE COULD SEEM USELESS AND FURTHERMORE COMPLETELY OUTDATED. IN COMPARISON TO TRACTORS OR MODERN CARS, IT IS UNDENIABLE THAT FAR MORE HORSEPOWER IS ABLE TO RESIDE BENEATH THE HOOD OF ANY VEHICLE THAN IN AN

ENTIRE STABLE. HOWEVER, COMPARING REAL HORSES WITH ENGINE POWER IS A POINTLESS EXERCISE, FOR THE POWER OF HORSES IS STILL USEFUL, BUT FOR VERY DIFFERENT PURPOSES, NOW MORE PSYCHOLOGICAL THAN MECHANICAL. IF WE CONSIDER THE WORLD OF HORSES TODAY, WE CAN SAY THAT THEY ARE MORE VALUABLE THAN EVER TO MAN'S EGO. IT IS NO LONGER TERRITORIES THAT WE CONQUER ON HORSEBACK, BUT PRIZES, AWARDS, HONORS, THE RECOGNITION OF OUR PEERS, AND SOMETIMES EVEN MONEY, LOTS OF MONEY. THE HORSE'S ATHLETIC STRENGTH AND POTENTIAL IS STILL AT MAN'S SERVICE, NO LONGER TO FEED OR TRANSPORT HIM, BUT TO HELP HIM AND TO SERVE HIM AS A SOURCE OF AMUSEMENT.

CONSEQUENTLY, IT IS TEMPTING TO ASSUME THAT A HORSE'S LIFE ITSELF HAS, BY EXTENSION, BECOME ONE OF LEISURE. IN COMPARISON TO ITS PAST, BENEATH HEAVY ARMOR OR IN THE MINES, THE LIFE OF A SPORTS MOUNT SEEMS ALMOST LAZY AND ENVIABLY COMFORTABLE. HOWEVER, THIS CONCLUSION IS INCORRECT IN MANY RESPECTS, FOR THE LIFE THAT WE IMPOSE ON OUR COMPETITION HORSES IS UNNATURAL AND SOMETIMES MORE DESTRUCTIVE FOR THEM THAN PROPERLY REGULATED HEAVY WORK.

FORTUNATELY, IN RECENT YEARS THE HORSE'S STRENGTH AND DAZZLING ENERGY HAVE FOUND A NEW USE AT MAN'S SERVICE. NO MORE CONQUESTS, PARADES OR OUTDATED TASKS: THE HORSE IS NOW USED TO FULFILL PART OF OUR HUMANITY, OUR WISH TO COMMUNICATE WITH THE LIVING AND TO FUEL OUR OWN ENERGY.

THIS SPECIAL HARMONIOUS RELATIONSHIP HAS ALWAYS EXISTED, AND MYTHS AND LEGENDS FROM ALL OVER THE WORLD RECOUNT THE COMMUNION BETWEEN MAN AND HIS MOUNTS. HOWEVER, IN THE PAST THEY WERE ADDRESSED AT INITIATES, PEOPLE WHO WERE VERY FAMILIAR WITH HORSES AND LIVED INTIMATELY WITH THEM. TODAY ANYONE – OR ALMOST ANYONE – CAN EXPERIENCE THIS EXCHANGE. THE MOVEMENT KNOWN AS THE HORSE WHISPERERS (TRAINERS WHO USE AN APPROACH BASED ON THE HORSE'S POINT OF VIEW, CENTERED ON COMMUNICATION AND NON-VIOLENCE – TRANSLATOR'S NOTE) HAS PAVED THE WAY FOR AMATEURS. "SUNDAY RIDERS" CAN NOW ACHIEVE A MASTERY OF THE HORSE SIMPLY, NATURALLY AND PACIFICALLY, ALLOWING THEM TO CHANNEL ITS POWER IN A TRUE PARTNERSHIP ACCOMPANIED BY RESPECT, MUTUAL UNDERSTANDING AND INTELLIGENCE.

THIS NEW RULE IS APPLIED INDEPENDENT OF THE SETTING: FORCE IS USED INCREASINGLY RARELY, REPLACED INSTEAD BY COMPREHENSION. CONSEQUENTLY, WOMEN OCCUPY A NEW POSITION IN VARIOUS DISCIPLINES IN THE EQUESTRIAN WORLD. TODAY WOMEN RIDERS INCREASINGLY OFTEN WIN THE TOP PRIZES. AS THEY ARE UNABLE TO PIT THEIR PHYSICAL STRENGTH AGAINST

80-81   The Friesian is a concentrate of power and energy.

83   This young Lusitano has just been released in the ring following hours
of waiting in his stable.

THAT OF THE HORSE, THEY HAVE ALWAYS DEVELOPED A SENSE OF COLLABO-

RATION AND AFFECTION. AFTER HAVING ACHIEVED THE DESIRED PERFORM-

ANCE, THE TRAINER TRIES TO MOTIVATE RATHER THAN FORCE THE ANIMAL,

CHANNELING ITS STRENGTH RATHER THAN CONSUMING IT BRUTALLY. IN-

DEED, THERE ARE NOW MORE WOMEN RIDERS THAN EVER IN THE TOP TEN

WORLD CHAMPIONSHIPS IN ALL DISCIPLINES.

ENDURANCE RIDING IS UNDOUBTEDLY ONE OF THE MOST STRENUOUS

ACTIVITIES FOR THE HORSE. INTERNATIONAL COMPETITIONS COVER A DAILY

DISTANCE OF 100 MILES, OVER VARIOUS TERRAINS: SLOPING, STONY AND

SANDY. THE HORSES MANAGE TO MAINTAIN AN AVERAGE SPEED BETWEEN

10.5 AND 12.5 MILES PER HOUR. THIS ENTAILS HOURS OF GALLOPING WITH AN

ADULT RIDER. THEY HAVE A FEW SHORT RESTS DURING THE RACE AND ARE

WATERED AT REGULAR INTERVALS. NONETHELESS, THE EVENT IS VERY CHAL-

LENGING, FAR MORE SO THAN THE MARATHONS RUN BY MEN, WHO ARE UN-

ABLE TO SUSTAIN THE EFFORT FOR MORE THAN 3 OR 4 HOURS, AND WHO ARE

NOT CARRYING ANYTHING ON THEIR BACKS.

HORSES ARE PERFECT ATHLETES. NOT ONLY DO THEY HAVE GREAT

STAMINA, BUT THEY ARE ALSO INCREDIBLY FAST. MOST HORSES CAN GALLOP

AT SPEEDS OF UP TO 28 MPH (20 KM/HR), WHILE THOROUGHBREDS CAN

REACH AN AVERAGE SPEED OF 35 MPH (56 KM/PH) OVER DISTANCES EXCEED-

power and energy

ING 1.25 MILES (2 KM) AND SOME HAVE EVEN REACHED A TOP SPEED OF 44 MPH (70 KM/HR).

WHERE DO HORSES FIND ALL THIS ENERGY THAT SO FASCINATES MAN? IT IS PRINCIPALLY THE RESULT OF EVOLUTION: 60 MILLION YEARS HAVE ELAPSED AND THE HORSE HAS BEEN ABLE TO SURVIVE THE ATTACKS OF ALMOST ALL ITS PREDATORS, CHIEFLY BY FLEEING THEM. INDEED, THE HORSE'S RESPONSIVENESS, LIVELINESS AND SPEED ARE THE KEY RESULTS OF THIS PROCESS OF NATURAL SELECTION. SUBSEQUENTLY MAN INTERVENED, MIXING THE ORIGINS, ADDING CHARACTERISTICS AND SPECIALIZING THE BREEDS ACCORDING TO THE POWER OR SPEED REQUIRED FOR VARIOUS PURPOSES, RESULTING IN SPRINTERS SUCH AS THE ENGLISH THOROUGHBRED, OR DRAFT HORSES SUCH AS THE PERCHERON AND THE SHIRE.

HOWEVER, IN ADDITION TO THEIR PURELY PHYSICAL ASPECTS, HORSES ALSO POSSESS A UNIQUE BLEND OF ENERGY, PRESENCE AND INCREDIBLY INTENSE VITALITY. WE HAVE NO RATIONAL EXPLANATION FOR THIS AND IT REMAINS A MYSTERY, AS DOES THE POTENTIAL OF EACH INDIVIDUAL AND HIS OR HER VITAL FORCE AND INBORN ASSETS. SOMETIMES A PERSON ENTERS A ROOM AND IMMEDIATELY ATTRACTS THE ATTENTION OF THE OTHERS. IT'S NOT A MATTER OF BEAUTY OR ORIGINALITY, BUT MERELY CHARISMA, AURA, AN INNER ENERGY THAT IS RADIATED TOWARD OTHERS. SUCH INDIVIDUALS ALSO EXIST IN THE EQUINE WORLD, EXERTING AN IRRESISTIBLE ATTRACTION AND LEAVING AN UNDYING MEMORY.

HAVE YOU EVER ATTENDED A HORSE SALE? NEXT TIME, TAKE A LOOK AT THE DESCRIPTIONS OF THE ANIMALS ON OFFER. THEY'RE ALL EXCELLENT HORSES, WELL BRED, PERFECTLY TRAINED AND IMPECCABLY TURNED OUT FOR THE OCCASION. EXAMINE THE CATALOG, PAGE BY PAGE, AND LOOK AT THE PHOTOGRAPHS OF THESE SPLENDID SPECIMENS. HOWEVER, WHEN THE ONE WHOSE DESCRIPTION YOU'VE JUST READ ENTERS THE RING, YOU MAY SUDDENLY FORGET ABOUT THE CATALOG, THE PUBLIC, THE PRESENTER AND THE SALE. TIME STANDS STILL AND YOUR HEART SEEMS TO STOP BEATING.

YOU'RE AWARE ONLY OF THE HORSE'S BEAUTY AND INDESCRIBABLE ENERGY, THE POWER EMANATED NOT ONLY BY HIS BODY, BUT ALSO BY HIS SOUL. IT'S LIKE FALLING IN LOVE, AND YOU PHYSICALLY NEED THE HORSE. YOU NEED TO ENVELOP YOURSELF IN THE SENSATION THAT HE EMANATES, AND YOU'RE UNABLE TO LET HIM OUT OF YOUR LIFE AND INTO THAT OF SOMEBODY ELSE. IT'S NOT A QUESTION OF THE HORSE'S VALUE, BECAUSE THIS LOVE-AT-FIRST-SIGHT EXPERIENCE CAN ALSO OCCUR AT A VILLAGE LIVESTOCK FAIR. INSTEAD IT'S THE ANIMAL'S ENERGY, VIBRATIONS AND RESONANCE THAT ATTRACT YOU. WHEN YOU FIND THIS DOUBLE, THIS STEED IN WHICH YOU FALL HEAD OVER HEELS IN LOVE, THEN YOU'LL KNOW WHAT IT MEANS TO LIVE WITHIN A HORSE'S ENERGY. YOUR INNER FORCE IS FUELED BY HIS PRESENCE, YOUR SILENT DIALOGUES AND YOUR ESCAPADES BRING YOU TOGETHER. THE MARVELOUS PRESENCE OF YOUR HORSE WILL COMFORT AND REGENERATE YOU, RELIEVING YOUR WORRIES AND THE BURDEN OF EVERYDAY LIFE. AN HOUR ON HIS BACK, OR SIMPLY BY HIS SIDE, WILL CAUSE YOUR PROBLEMS TO DISAPPEAR MIRACULOUSLY WITHOUT A TRACE. YOU'LL RETURN FROM THE STABLES HAPPY, RELAXED, CAREFREE AND BRIMMING WITH A MYSTERIOUS ENERGY WHOSE SECRET ORIGIN IS KNOWN TO YOU ALONE.

power and energy

84-85   Everything in Iceland is charged with an indomitable force: the volcanic land, the rugged beauty of the landscape and the herds of horses that gallop over the wild island.

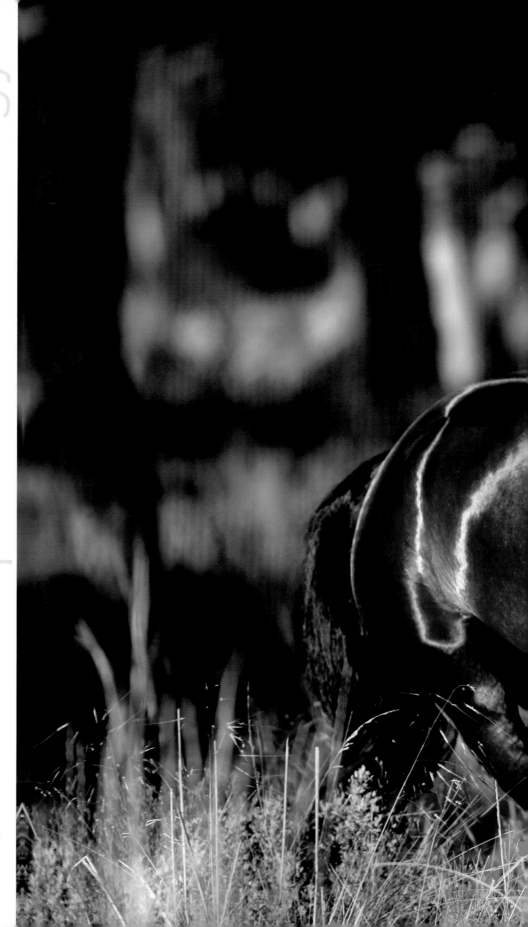

86-87 Naïpe is a Lusitano, a breed that combines
extraordinary power and gentleness. He is magnificent at
work, as he conscientiously prepares for Grand Prix dressage,
but equally handsome when roaming free in the Andalusian
scrub. His common sense is matched by his great power.

power and energy

89   I've always been fascinated by Friesians. They look as though they have stepped straight out of a Baroque painting, and are very photogenic horses. Apart from the Netherlands, of course, I also seek my finest models in Germany and the United States.

90-91, 92 and 93 Could this excited creature possibly be a reincarnation of the devil? With its shiny black coat and mane flying in all directions, the great body positively exudes energy. Seeing it like this, who would guess that this one of the gentlest and most tranquil horses once inside the stable?

94 and 95   Templado performs his act. This Spanish stallion is one of the most handsome creatures that I know, as well as an uncommon and very lovable personality. It is no surprise that Frédéric Pignon's show horse has become an international star, from the United States to Germany, not to mention France.

power and energy

96, 97 and 98-99   The thrill of freedom, movement and energy that can finally flow unhindered. Horses are born for a life of constant movement, but today they are often transformed into overfed and inactive animals confined to a loose box. When I photograph them I always ask their owners to release them in a wide open space. This allows me to take shots of horses that radiate joy – while their owners panic as they watch them vent their energy! I often secretly tell myself that, even if I might not have taken the photo of the century, at least my visit has allowed the horses to rediscover the taste of freedom for a few moments.

100-101   A race between Gypsy Vanners: the winner is the first to cross the imaginary finishing line at the end of the field. Horses love galloping like this, shoulder to shoulder, striving to outrun their neighbors and pretending to bite them if they dare overtake them.

102-103   Over 1323 lbs (600 kg) of pure muscle combined with the nimbleness of a mountain goat: the paradox of the horse is explained by its compact mass that allows it to defy the laws of gravity.

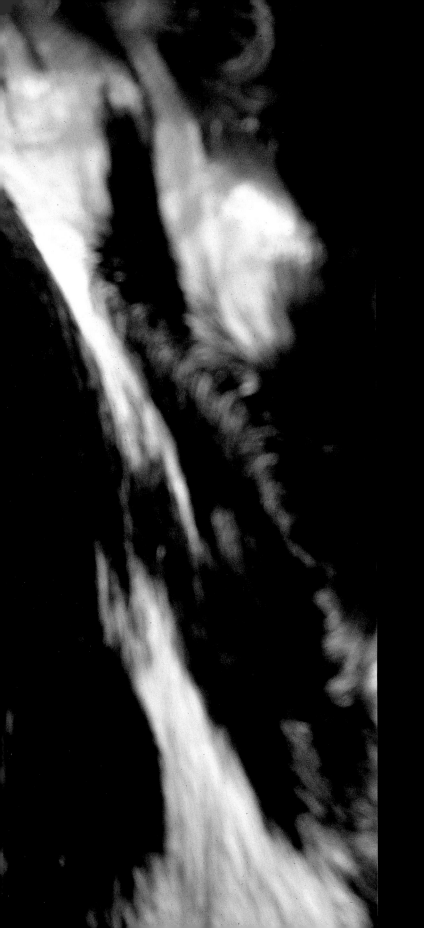

104-105   The power and depth of the gaze of a Criollo stallion, immortalized on the Argentinian pampas. Responsible for a great herd of mares and foals, he immedi placed himself before me to make it clear who was in charge: I could only do wh permitted with his family.

power and energy

106-107   A vigorous neck and a long mane, with a strong and powerful head: the
Friesian has inherited many of the qualities of its Spanish ancestors, which were used
to refine the bloodstock of the ebony-coated mares. The breed has always placed its
beauty and strength at the service of man, first as a war horse, then as farm horse and
now a show horse.

108-109 and 110-111 When an entire herd of Argentinian Criollos gallops across the pampas toward you, the first thing that you notice is the vibration of the ground beneath your feet, before sighting a great cloud of dust. A few seconds later, when the drumming sound has become deafening, the horses suddenly appear in front of you like a wall. They swerve slightly to avoid you, and you will find yourself in the midst of a rushing, swollen river, dazed by the speed and noise of the flow. Then they disappear, followed by the cloud. The vibrations gradually cease. Was it just a vision?

112-113 Splashing in water is a great treat for horses that are used to it, which also enjoy galloping on the seashore or bathing in a river. Horses often enter water of their own accord during very hot weather, cooling their legs and bellies or using their hooves to splash themselves.

114 As the Friesian stallion Pandur was walking along a
North Sea beach at sunset, a seagull flew past the camera
and into the picture. I'll never forget that photo shoot:
Pandur was such a willing model that we spent a long time
working together. It was a truly extraordinary experience.

116-117   The little Icelandic pony is a surprising concentrate of power. Although no taller than 13 hands at the withers, these animals are capable of carrying an adult man over 60 miles (100 km) without batting an eyelid. These descendents of the Viking horses are exceptionally hardy and the noble heirs of an extremely pure line.

118-119   These Arabian mares enjoy galloping along the shores of the North Sea and splashing through the waves, up to their bellies in the water.

120-121   The air is icy (c. 14 °F/ -10 °C) and the snow reaches the horse's knees, but they nonetheless seem perfectly at ease galloping through the Wyoming snow.

ach State Stud in Germany released on the fresh
e horses, which have been shut up for a while, are
until, dripping with sweat and panting, they finally
er and return to the stables, happy and relaxed.

124-125   Haflingers are accustomed to dealing with the powdery snow on the Alpine slopes. The surprising liveliness and high spirits of these Austrian ponies can be explained by their Arabian blood.

power and energy

127   I had the wall behind my stables painted Andalusian yellow in order to bring a little Spanish sun to the long, gray German winter and, most importantly, because it provides the ideal backdrop for the silhouette of horses in motion, like this Friesian, whose black coat is normally very difficult to photograph.

128-129   The liveliness and mobility of purebred Arabians are unrivaled among horses. This one pirouettes before my eyes and performs a series of well-controlled sliding stops and turns on the hindquarters with amazing agility.

130 and 131 Is it a dance, a fight, or simply a game? This young horse expresses its irrepressible need to let its exuberance and imagination run free in a display of harmonious acrobatics. Onlookers may feel frightened (in the case of novices), flattered by his beauty (in the case of his owner), or simply amused and touched by the young stallion's impetuosity.

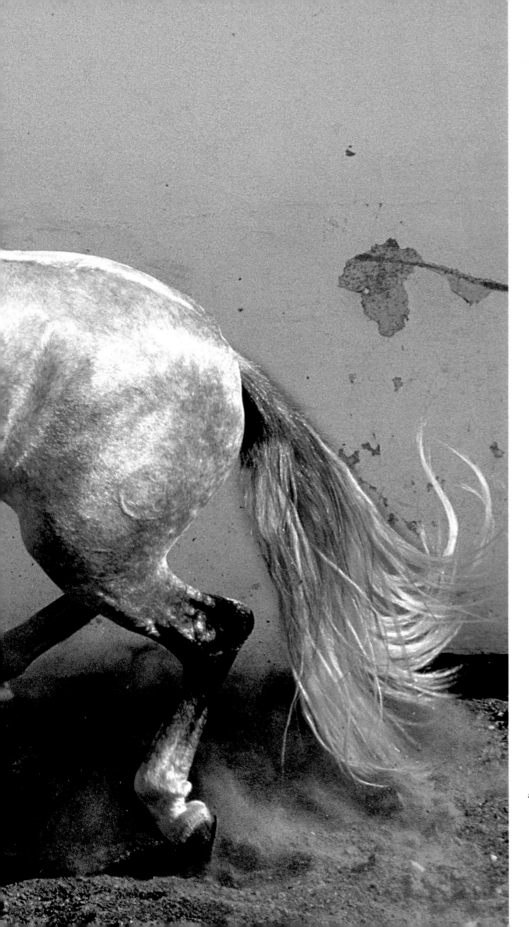

132-133   This athletic horse is not actually challenging anything or anyone. He is simply playing with space and his lithe, tonic body, savoring the basic, yet vital, pleasure of movement. And perhaps he also wishes to surprise the onlookers crowding the terraces, for he loves showing off, demonstrating what he is capable of and impressing the public. He is both an athlete and a jester.

134-135 Sometimes I shut horses in their loose boxes for a few hours in order to be sure that I capture those few moments during which they angrily work off their pent-up energy when they are finally released. The burst of energy only lasts around five minutes, after which the horse is once again in form but less explosive – and thus less photogenic.

136-137 The nobility of a Baroque horse, forthright, powerful and agile: only the Iberian breeds are able to incarnate such beauty, characterized above all by an arched neck and a thick mane.

138-139 Purebred Arabians are distinguished by their refined elegance and vibrant energy: the Bedouins call them the "Drinkers of the Wind," in tribute to their airy movements and unmatched stamina.

curiosity and fun

curiosity and fun

EACH TIME THAT I VISIT A HERD OF FREE HORSES, GOING ABOUT THEIR DAILY LIVES IN A FIELD OR A CORRAL, I ALWAYS

END UP MAKING THE ACQUAINTANCE OF THE CLOWN OF THE GROUP. HE'S NEVER THE FIRST TO GREET YOU, NOR CAN

HE BE DISTINGUISHED FROM THE OTHER MEMBERS OF THE GROUP BY HIS HIERARCHICAL POSITION. AT FIRST SIGHT HE'S

LOST IN THE MASS, BUT SOONER OR LATER HE STEPS FORWARD. WHEN YOUR MIND'S ELSEWHERE, A NOSE ARRIVES FROM

BEHIND TO NUDGE YOUR SHOULDER, MUSS UP YOUR HAIR OR NIBBLE THE HEM OF YOUR JACKET. THE CLOWN IS DYING

OF CURIOSITY, BUT IF YOU TURN ROUND TO FACE HIM, HE'LL LEAP BACK AND HURRY TO HIDE AMONG THE OTHERS. HE'S

NOT BRAVE BUT HE HAS AN INCREDIBLE DESIRE TO GET TO KNOW YOU, TO DISCOVER WHO YOU ARE AND TO SMELL YOU.

THE OTHER HORSES WATCH YOU FROM A SAFE DISTANCE, REMAINING TOGETHER. IF THEY DECIDE THAT YOU DON'T

POSE A THREAT AND WON'T HURT THEM OR TRY TO CATCH THEM, THEY'LL PUT THEIR NOSES BACK TO THE GROUND AND

PEACEFULLY RESUME GRAZING AFTER A FEW MINUTES. BUT NOT THE CLOWN: HE'LL BECOME YOUR SHADOW AND FOL-

LOW YOUR EVERY ACTION AND MOVEMENT, TO THE EXTENT THAT YOU NEED TO KEEP YOUR EYE ON HIM. MINE STARTS

BY SCATTERING THE ENTIRE CONTENTS OF MY WORKBAG: FILM CANISTERS, LENSES AND FILMS, UNTIL HE HAS RE-

ARRANGED THEM TO HIS LIKING. AND WHEN IT HAPPENS TO BE A YOUNG STALLION, HE EVEN MAY TRY TO MOUNT ME,

JUST TO PLAY AT WHO IS THE STRONGEST. THIS IS PERFECTLY NORMAL, FOR IT'S WHAT HE DOES WITH HIS COMPANIONS

OF THE SAME AGE! THERE IS NO MALICE IN HIS EYES, JUST MISCHIEF, GREAT INTELLIGENCE AND THE MARVELOUS INNO-

CENCE OF CHILDHOOD.

IF YOU PAY ATTENTION TO THE CLOWN AND GET TO KNOW HIM WELL, HE MAKES A FANTASTIC PHOTOGRAPHER'S

MODEL. HE REACTS IMMEDIATELY TO EVERYTHING YOU DO, ENJOYING HIMSELF AND SOMETIMES ADDING HIS OWN CON-

TRIBUTIONS, SUCH AS CHASING YOU! HOWEVER, AT A CERTAIN POINT YOU HAVE TO REMIND HIM THAT YOU'RE NOT A

HORSE. EVEN IF YOU'RE A PLAYFUL AND FUN-LOVING PERSON, YOU CAN'T ENJOY ALL HIS GAMES. IF YOU FORGET TO TELL

HIM TO STOP BEFORE IT'S TOO LATE, THEN YOU'D BETTER START WORRYING! IT'S LIKE ALLOWING A CHILD TO BECOME

OVER-EXCITED AND RUN OUT OF CONTROL WHILE PLAYING. SOMETIMES THE RESULTS CAN BE DANGEROUS, I.E., PAINFUL,

WITH A LITTLE IMP WEIGHING FROM CA. 20 TO 40 LBS (10 TO 20 KG) ON THE RAMPAGE, SO JUST IMAGINE FOR A MOMENT

THE SAME SITUATION WITH A CA. 900-LBS (400 KG) RASCAL WHO IS A CONCENTRATE OF MUSCLES AND ENERGY! JUST LIKE

A CURIOUS AND PLAYFUL CHILD, THE CLOWN TESTS YOUR AUTHORITY AND NEVER TAKES ANYTHING FOR GRANTED. IT'S

UP TO YOU TO SET THE LIMITS.

IF A HORSE LIKE THIS ENTERS YOUR LIFE, EXPECT TO FIND HIM REGULARLY OUTSIDE HIS PADDOCK ON THE LAWN, BE-

CAUSE HE WAS OVERWHELMED BY THE URGE TO EXPLORE THE NEIGHBOR'S GARDEN. CLOSE THE DOORS UNLESS YOU

WANT TO FIND HIM IN THE KITCHEN OR THE LIVING ROOM, AND FENCE OFF PONDS OR LAKES BEFORE YOU HAVE TO GO

AND FISH HIM OUT. THE BEST WAY TO STOP HIM FROM DOING SOMETHING SILLY IS TO OFFER HIM ACTIVITIES THAT YOU

ARE ABLE TO CONTROL. JUST LIKE A GIFTED CHILD, IT'S A CHALLENGE TO FIND HIM NEW TOYS AND TEACH HIM NEW

THINGS ALL THE TIME. HE'S BORED BY ANYTHING REPETITIVE. WHAT'S MORE, IF YOU GET OFF TO A BAD START OR TAKE

140   The joy of rediscovering freedom after hours of confinement in a stable.

142 left and center   Colts at play.

142 right   These three young Arabians are curious to know what's going on.

143   Two young troublemakers learn to fight by playing.

THINGS TOO FAR, THE CLOWN BECOMES DISCOURAGED, AND THINKS "THAT'S ENOUGH, I DON'T WANT TO PLAY ANY MORE," AND DUMPS YOU!

THESE HORSES ARE ONLY HAPPY IF THEY FIND A GOOD PARTNER WITH WHOM TO SHARE THEIR MOMENTS OF IMAGINATION AND JOY, SOMEONE CAPABLE OF STIMULATING THEIR CURIOSITY. IF YOU PUT THEM OUT TO PASTURE WITH A BORING COMPANION, THEY WILL WASTE AWAY BEFORE YOUR EYES. IF THEY ARE RIDDEN BY PERSON OF BRUSQUE, INSENSITIVE HABITS, THEY WILL GRADUALLY DECLINE, BECOMING SHORT-TEMPERED AND SKITTISH. HORSES OFTEN HAVE A BETTER SENSE OF HUMOR AND MORE IMAGINATION THAN THEIR OWNERS.

PLAYING WITH A HORSE MAY SEEM STRANGE AND ENIGMATIC TO THOSE WHO ARE NOT FAMILIAR WITH THESE ANIMALS. HOWEVER, IT IS SUFFICIENT TO LISTEN TO WHAT HE WHISPERS IN YOUR EAR WHEN YOU GO TO LOOK FOR HIM IN HIS FIELD OR WHEN YOU RELEASE HIM IN THE STABLE PADDOCK AND HE PROVOKES YOU WITH HIS INVITATIONS FOR A GALLOP; OR DURING A RIDE, WHEN HE EYES UP A GRASSY AVENUE AND SEEMS TO SUGGEST A CANTER DOWN IT; OR ON A SPRING DAY WHEN HE'S FEELING IN PARTICULARLY GOOD FORM AND BEGS YOU TO LET HIM TO RELEASE HIS ENERGY A LITTLE; OR WHEN HE AFFECTIONATELY AND KNOWINGLY ASKS WHAT YOU'VE HIDDEN IN YOUR POCKET.

I ONCE HAD A HORSE WHO LIKED TO PLAY AT UNDRESSING ME. HE WAS HAPPY IN THE WINTER WHEN I ARRIVED BUNDLED UP IN A BIG JACKET FASTENED WITH LITTLE BUTTONS AND A LONG ZIPPER. AS SOON AS I WENT TO GREET HIM, HE'D DELICATELY GRASP THE BUTTONS, ONE BY ONE, AND SEVER THE THREAD WITH HIS TEETH, FROM TOP TO BOTTOM, WITH METICULOUS CARE. ONCE HE'D CONSCIENTIOUSLY REMOVED THE ROW OF BUTTONS, HIS LIPS WOULD NUZZLE MY NECK UNTIL HE'D FOUND THE ZIPPER. HE'D TICKLE MY NECK, MAKING ME LAUGH, BUT REFUSED TO LET HIMSELF BE DISTRACTED. IN JUST A FEW SECONDS HE'D FIND WHAT HE WAS LOOKING FOR AND UNDO MY JACKET COMPLETELY. HE'D THEN THRUST HIS NOSE INSIDE AND WE'D LAUGH TOGETHER. THIS RITUAL COST ME SEVERAL MENDING SESSIONS, BUT JUST AS MANY MOMENTS OF PURE HAPPINESS.

DURING THE SUMMER WE HAD TO FIND OTHER GAMES, BUT IT WASN'T DIFFICULT. WE LOVED TO PLAY AT TAKING TURNS, FOR EXAMPLE I'D CHOOSE ONE PATH AND HE'D CHOOSE THE NEXT ONE. AND IF I TRIED TO BREAK THE RULE, HE'D CONSIDER IT A REAL BETRAYAL! THE PROBLEM WAS THAT MY DEAR FRIEND LOVED GOING FOR RIDES AND EACH TIME THAT I TRIED TO TURN BACK TOWARD THE STABLE, HE'D BLATANTLY TAKE THE OPPOSITE DIRECTION AS SOON AS IT WAS HIS TURN. THE GAME COULD LAST UNTIL NIGHTFALL AND ENDED UP WORRYING OTHER PEOPLE, WHO OF COURSE

KNEW NOTHING ABOUT OUR ECCENTRICITIES. THIS HORSE ALSO PROVED TO ME THAT HE WAS PERFECTLY CAPABLE OF UNDERSTANDING PEOPLE'S GAMES. I USED TO THINK THAT I HAD TO OBSERVE HIM IN ORDER TO FIND A WAY TO COMMUNICATE, BUT HE OFTEN SHOWED ME THAT HE WAS ABLE TO DO EXACTLY THE SAME THING, OBSERVING ME AND ADAPTING HIMSELF TO PLAY WITH ME. ONE DAY WHILE I WAS ORGANIZING A GAME FOR CHILDREN ON PONIES, MY HORSE WAS NEAR US, FREE AS USUAL. IT DIDN'T TAKE HIM LONG TO UNDERSTAND THAT YOU NEEDED TO STAND ON THE STARTING LINE, AT THE FAR END OF THE RING, AND THEN GALLOP TO THE OTHER END TO SEIZE A WHIP HELD IN A CLAMP. WHEN THE THIRD RACE STARTED WE HAD A NEW COMPETITOR, WITHOUT A RIDER, WHO HAD INVITED HIMSELF TO PLAY. OF COURSE, HE GRABBED THE PRIZE EVERY SINGLE TIME, WHILE THE ASTONISHED CHILDREN SHOUTED, "YOU'RE A REAL CROOK, BALTHAZAR!" IT WAS THE FIRST TIME THAT I SAW CHILDREN LOSE A GAME SO HAPPILY.... THAT EPISODE REALLY ALLOWED ME TO UNDERSTAND THE EXTENT TO WHICH A HORSE CAN BECOME A COMPANION AND AN ACCOMPLICE.

HOWEVER, SOMETIMES THE EQUINE SENSE OF HUMOR CAN BECOME TOO MUCH, FOR HORSES CAN TAKE THEIR TRICKS TOO FAR. I REMEMBER A MARE THAT OFTEN PLAYED AT FRIGHTENING PEOPLE THAT SHE DISLIKED. THE PROBLEM WAS THAT THE YOUNG LADY WAS EXTREMELY SELECTIVE . . .

TO THE EXTENT THAT ONE PERSON IN TWO WAS SUBJECTED TO HER GAMES. HER FAVORITE ONE WAS PREVENTING THEM FROM CATCHING THEIR MOUNTS IN THE PADDOCK. SHE'D STAND BETWEEN THEM AND THEIR HORSES AND PROVOKE THEM, AS THOUGH SAYING, "WELL, IF YOU WANT TO CATCH THEM, GIVE IT A TRY!" AND THREATENING THEM BY FLATTENING HER EARS AND KEEPING BETWEEN THEM WHEN THEY SOUGHT A WAY OUT. AND INDEED, A FAIR NUMBER OF PEOPLE GAVE UP THE IDEA OF A RIDE, SECRETLY ASHAMED OF THEMSELVES. I DISCOVERED HER TRICK ONE DAY, WHEN A POOR BREATHLESS, DISHEVELED AND PRACTICALLY DESPERATE RIDER RETURNED TO THE STABLE EMPTY-HANDED AND STUTTERINGLY ASKED ME IF I COULD PLEASE CATCH HIS HORSE IN THE PADDOCK. GIVEN HIS STATE, I DIDN'T ASK ANY QUESTIONS. HE POINTED OUT HIS MOUNT FROM AFAR AND STAYED AT THE EDGE OF THE CORRAL, AS THOUGH TERRIFIED. I PICKED UP THE HALTER AND WALKED TOWARD THE ANIMAL, PAUSING TO GIVE A KISS ON THE NOSE TO THE SHE-DEVIL, WHO DIDN'T BAT AN EYE. WHEN I TOOK HIM HIS HORSE, THE RIDER LOOKED AT ME IN AMAZEMENT, ASKING, "SHE LET YOU PASS?" I IMMEDIATELY UNDERSTOOD WHOM HE WAS REFERRING TO AND SMILED TO MYSELF. THAT SMILE WAS FOR THE MARE. I AGREED WITH HER ENTIRELY: THAT MAN WASN'T IN THE LEAST BIT LIKEABLE!

THE MOST MOVING THING FOR ME IS TO WATCH HORSES PLAYING TO-

144   This foal uses his mother's tail as a flywhisk.

146-147   Horses adore rolling in the sand, enjoying a back massage accompanied by a dry bath in a moment of pure happiness.

149   This pony is making a strange face, not to make us laugh, but in order to discern certain smells more accurately.

150-151   An Icelandic stallion shakes his head to tell one of the mares to move. He stands behind her, moving so that she goes where he wants.

GETHER. THE YOUNGER THEY ARE, THE MORE TIME THEY DEDICATE TO PLAY, IN WHICH THEY INVEST AN OVERWHELMING AMOUNT OF ENERGY. IN THE CASE OF FOALS, THIS MEANS CONSTANT CLOWNERY. THEY TRY TO MOUNT EACH OTHER AND CHASE EACH OTHER AT A WILD GALLOP, THROWING THEIR LONG LEGS OUT IN ALL DIRECTIONS, AS THOUGH PARTICIPATING IN A GYMNASTICS EVENT OR A DANCE. AS THEY GROW, THEIR GAMES BECOME MORE VIRILE, ESPECIALLY IN THE CASE OF COLTS, BUT THE MUTUAL UNDER-STANDING DOES NOT DISAPPEAR AND THE FIGHTS, ALTHOUGH SPECTACU-LAR, ARE ALWAYS PERFECTLY CONTROLLED. THE MAIN GAME OF ADULTS CONSISTS OF DELIGHTFUL GALLOPS. ONE OF THEM TWITCHES HIS NOS-TRILS, AND RESTLESSLY PAWS THE GROUND, BEFORE CHARGING IF HE SENS-ES INTEREST AMONG THE OTHERS. THEN THE HERD SUDDENLY TAKES OFF, LIKE A FLOCK OF BIRDS, ACCOMPANIED BY A HUGE ROLL ON THE DRUMS. THE VIBRATING EARTH AND SOUND OF HOOVES DURING ONE OF THESE FU-RIOUS GALLOPS IS ENOUGH TO SEND A SHIVER DOWN THE SPINE OF "CIVI-LIZED" PEOPLE AND ALSO TO MAKE WILD RIDERS – THE DESCENDENTS OF GENGHIS KHAN – TWITCH WITH EXCITEMENT.

OUR HORSES WILL ONLY BE TRULY OLD WHEN THEY CEASE BEING CURI-OUS ABOUT EVERYTHING, WISHING TO SHOVE THEIR NOSES EVERYWHERE AND SEIZING EACH CHANCE FOR PLAY. FORTUNATELY, THIS USUALLY HAP-

curiosity and fun

PENS VERY LATE IN LIFE AND FOR SOME – THOSE WHO DIE OF OLD AGE STILL CONVINCED THAT THEY ARE FOALS – THE MOMENT NEVER COMES. THE SADDEST THING TO SEE IS A HORSE THAT DOES NOT PLAY AND REMAINS IDLE EVEN IN THE PRIME OF LIFE. THIS IS SHEER FOLLY, AN ABERRATION THAT OFFENDS THE EQUINE RACE, BUT IT IS NONETHELESS THE DEPRESSING LIFE OF MANY HORSES, THOSE THAT WE CONSIDER THE MOST SPOILED AND PAMPERED. WE FIND THESE UNHAPPY BEASTS IN SMART STABLES WHERE CARE HAS BEEN TAKEN TO SEPARATE THE LOOSE BOXES, WHERE THE ENCLOSURES CONTAIN ONLY SAND, AND WHERE THE IDEA OF PUTTING A HORSE OUT TO GRASS, ESPECIALLY WITH OTHERS OF ITS GROUP, IS NEVER EVEN CONTEMPLATED.

THESE ANIMALS, CONSIDERED TOO HANDSOME OR TOO SUCCESSFUL TO LEAD A HORSE'S LIFE, ARE MORTALLY BORED, SOMETIMES FALLING SICK AS A RESULT. PLAY AND THE JOY OF DISCOVERY HAVE DISAPPEARED FROM THEIR LIVES, WHICH IS TRAGIC FOR THESE ETERNAL CHILDREN. THE MORE IMAGINATIVE INDIVIDUALS STILL FIND A WAY OF HAVING A LITTLE FUN BETWEEN THE FOUR WALLS: SOME GRAB THEIR BUCKET AND FLING IT INTO THE AIR LIKE A BALL, WHILE OTHERS DISCOVER HOW TO OPEN EVEN THE STURDIEST BOLT OF THEIR BOXES WITH THEIR NOSES. MANUFACTURERS HAVE EVEN INVENTED SPECIAL TOYS, IN THE FORM OF VARIOUS KINDS OF BALLS, WHICH ALLOW "CIVILIZED" HORSES TO OCCUPY THE 22 HOURS OF THE DAY THAT THEY SPEND LOCKED UP.

STABLE TOYS! WHAT HAVE WE DONE TO OUR POOR HORSES? AFTER CENTURIES SPENT ON THE BATTLEFIELD, AMID THE MUD AND BLOOD, THE PEACEFUL HORSE WE NOW HAVE, PROJECTED INTO A STERILIZED WORLD, WHERE IT IS ISOLATED AND SUBJECTED TO THE LAWS OF CONSUMER SOCIETY.

PREVENTING A HORSE FROM EXPLORING, HAVING FUN AND CONTINUOUSLY LEARNING MEANS DENYING NOT ONLY HIS TRUE NATURE, BUT ALSO FORGETTING THE BASES OF OUR SHARED HISTORY. OVER 5000 YEARS AGO MAN WAS ABLE TO DOMESTICATE THE HORSE PRINCIPALLY DUE TO ITS GREED AND CURIOSITY.

HOWEVER, HISTORIANS AND ETHNOLOGISTS ARE A NOW ALMOST CERTAIN: HORSES CHOSE TO LET THEMSELVES BE DOMESTICATED – UNLIKE OTHER MEMBERS OF THE SAME FAMILY SUCH AS ZEBRAS – JUST AS WE CHOSE THEM. WHY? BECAUSE WE AROUSED THEIR CURIOSITY AND WERE ALSO ABLE TO ENSURE THEM TWO FUNDAMENTAL NEEDS: FOOD AND PROTECTION AGAINST PREDATORS. THE NOBLEST CONQUEST THUS OCCURRED WITH THEIR CONSENT, AND THIS ENCOUNTER MAY EVEN HAVE BEEN PROVOKED BY THE HORSE ITSELF, DUE TO ITS CURIOSITY AND OPPORTUNISM. IT SEEMS LEGITIMATE TO ASK OURSELVES WHICH OF THE TWO CONQUERED THE OTHER....

IT WOULD BE A SERIOUS MISTAKE TO TAKE THIS INITIAL CONTRACT AND THIS BOND BETWEEN HORSE AND MAN FOR GRANTED. WE MUST ALWAYS BE AWARE OF OUR HORSE'S INTEREST AND THE REASONS FOR WHICH HE HAS CHOSEN US.

LIKE ANY LOVE STORY, IT CAN BE WONDERFUL, AS LONG AS WE BOTH CONTINUE TO SEDUCE EACH OTHER. IT'S DIFFICULT, BUT THE RESULT IS WORTH IT. IF WE TAKE THIS STEP TOWARD THE HORSE, HE WILL GO TO THE ENDS OF THE EARTH – WITH US, BUT ABOVE ALL FOR US.

152 and 153   Manes flowing in the wind like banners, these stallions seem as though they wish
to show off their fine looks and virility. Whether the wind is blowing in Iceland (left) or Spain
(right), the stallions' manes ripple proudly beneath the mares' noses.

154   This handsome Haflinger's curiosity is veiled by suspicion as I take his photograph.

155   The Flehmen response is a particular type of reaction that consists of closing the nostrils while curling the lips. It allows horses to isolate smells in order to analyze them better, particularly in the case of pheromones, which indicate the hormonal state of other males and females.

curiosity and fun

156-157 Hooves in the air: while this position may seem strange for a horse, these two roll several times a day to the great enjoyment of both.

158   Stallions such as this Icelandic pony must know how to prance, showing off to the mares, unless they want to see them disappear with another horse.

159   Young males practice the Flehmen response from an early age, curling their lips in order to decode the smells of their environment. Even newborn foals know that their sense of smell is vital for survival, and in particular for reproduction.

160   Nothing is more boring than a loose box for an animal born for wide open spaces
and life in a herd. When boxed, horses spend their time with their noses out of the window, in
order to see what's going on outside.

161   These two young horses are temporarily shut in their loose boxes, whose windows are
covered with canvas sheets. However, the need to see what's going on outside is far stronger
than the knot securing the fabric.

162 The Arabian's unrivaled grace is also evident in the way it thrusts its nose toward anything that arouses its curiosity. Safely behind the door of his loose box, this horse uses all his senses to perceive even the tiniest detail: ears pricked, nostrils dilated and eyes staring at the unknown object.

163 The horse's chief means of discovering the world is its nose. Firstly because smells constitute an essential source of information for identifying individuals and objects, and secondly because horses also use their noses like hands, for touching, feeling and moving things around them.

164 and 165   Horses have an impressive ability to note even the tiniest details and an astounding memory for them. They want to know everything that's going on, not just to feel safe, but also simply to pass the time. They know the hours and their related rituals. If even the tiniest detail of the daily life of the stable should change, then they become uneasy.

curiosity and fun

167   Ansata Nil Pacha, one of the finest French Arabian
stallions, enjoys a short ride in the ocher quarries of
sillon. His silver coat and white silken mane gleam in the
bright sunlight of Southern France.

168 This horse hidden behind the branches seems to be asking himself what's going on. He continues to graze, but monitors the slightest little movement.

168-169 Horses also use their mouths for discovery and pleasure. When they come across an unknown food, they either refuse it or eat a small quantity cautiously, in order to avoid the risk of poisoning. However, once they have discovered and enjoyed the taste of apples or pears, they won't miss the chance to eat them with relish.

curiosity and fun

170-171   These two superb Gypsy Vanners relax in each other's company. Like people, horses yawn when calm, relaxed and in a tranquil atmosphere – as shown by this individual, photographed alongside his favorite companion.

172   No, this horse is neither laughing nor neighing, but yawning!

173   No, this isn't a cheeky horse… just one that's tasted something new and wants to get rid of the flavor that has remained
in his mouth. Horses are very cautious with plants that they don't know, for fear of poisoning.
Indeed, many toxic species grow in their habitats.

174-175   This Friesian foal reveals his new teeth in a yawn
that announces a deep sleep.

curiosity and fun

176 and 177   The day after birth, this Quarter Horse foal already gallops like an adult
and discovers the taste of dandelions. He will not start grazing for a few weeks yet,
contenting himself with his mother's sweet milk in the meantime.

178 and 178-179   This Shetland pony foal has savored the great joys of being a horse from its very first days of life: the pleasure of galloping free and the delightful sensation of rolling on young grass. This pony will undoubtedly grow up to appreciate the finer things in life!

violence and fear

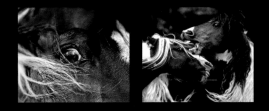

THE ONLY SOUND IS THE INCREDIBLE CRACK AND SLAP OF TWO BODIES VIOLENTLY COLLIDING. THE FIERCE AND BITTER STRUGGLE TAKES PLACE WITHOUT A CRY, LIKE A SILENT FILM IN WHICH THE ONLY SOUNDTRACK IS THAT OF THE CLASHES AND BLOWS.

THIS IS A FIGHT TO THE DEATH BETWEEN TWO STALLIONS. THE PIEBALD ONE IS OLDER AND MORE EXPERIENCED. HE ATTACKS THE YOUNGER ANIMAL MERCILESSLY WITH HIS HOOVES AND TEETH, LUNGING AT HIS ADVERSARY LIKE AN EXPERT BOXER PREPARING TO FLOOR AN AMATEUR IN THE RING. HOWEVER, THIS RING IS A CORRAL IN THE HEART OF THE ARGENTINIAN PAMPAS AND THE FIGHT HAS NO RULES OR LIMITS: ITS OUTCOME MAY BE FATAL. THE OPPONENTS HURL THEMSELVES AT EACH OTHER'S THROATS, USING ALL THEIR WEIGHT TO TRY TO KNOCK EACH OTHER OFF BALANCE, REARING UP AND THEN DROPPING BACK TO

THE GROUND, IN A CLOUD OF DUST. IT SEEMS AS THOUGH A CENTURY HAS PASSED SINCE THIS FASCINATING DUEL COMMENCED AND A SHIVER RUNS DOWN MY SPINE AS I CONTEMPLATE IT. PART OF ME IS UNABLE TO TEAR ITSELF AWAY FROM THIS WILD SPECTACLE, BOTH POWERFUL AND CRUEL, WHILE THE OTHER PART TREMBLES AT THE IDEA THAT ONE OF THE HORSES MAY BE KILLED AND WANTS TO CRY OUT TO STOP THE FIGHT.

INSTEAD I STAY WHERE I AM, MOTIONLESS LIKE THE REST OF THE HERD, WHERE THE FRIGHTENED FOALS HIDE BEHIND THEIR MOTHERS. THEY ARE ALL AWAITING THE OUTCOME OF THE FIGHT. THEY WANT TO KNOW THE WINNER, AND THUS THE LEADER WHO WILL COVER THE MARES AND TRANSMIT HIS GENES TO THE NEXT SEASON'S FOALS, DEFEND THEM FROM THE ATTACKS OF OUTSIDERS AND KEEP THE HERD TOGETHER IN THE COMING YEARS.

BLOOD FLOWS FREELY IN RIVULETS THROUGH THEIR SWEAT-SODDEN COATS. THEY ROLL THEIR EYES NERVOUSLY, THEIR TAILS FLICKING THE AIR; THE TENSION AND HOSTILITY ARE PALPABLE.

HOW DID THIS ALL START? THE YOUNG BLUE-EYED CRIOLLO STALLION HAD BEEN WAITING FOR THE RIGHT MOMENT FOR SEVERAL DAYS, FOLLOWING THE HERD AND BIDING HIS TIME FOR THE CHANCE TO BECOME ITS LEADER, REPLACING THE OLD PATRIARCH. HE'D BEEN WAITING FOR THE OPPORTUNITY TO PROVOKE AND CONFRONT HIM IN ORDER TO OUST HIM MORE EASILY. NOW THE DAY HAS COME. SPRING IS ALMOST HERE, AND THE MARES WILL SOON BE IN SEASON. THE YOUNG STALLION CAN WAIT NO LONGER: HIS INSTINCT, HORMONES AND GENES DRIVE HIM TO TRY HIS LUCK, AT THE COST OF RISKING HIS LIFE.

THE ARGENTINIAN GAUCHOS APPEAR TO OBSERVE THE SCENE WITH DETACHMENT, BUT THEIR EYES BETRAY THEIR TENSION AND AGITATION. THEY WILL NOT INTERVENE, EVEN IF IT BECOMES CLEAR THAT IT WILL END IN TRAGEDY, FOR THEY CONSIDER THE BLOODY DUEL A MEANS OF NATURAL SELECTION, WHOSE PURPOSE IS TO ELIMINATE THE WEAKER INDIVIDUAL TO MAKE WAY FOR THE STRONGER ONE. THEY WANT THE BEST AND STRONGEST STALLION TO WIN, IN ORDER TO ENSURE THAT THE CRIOLLO RETAINS ALL ITS CHARACTERISTICS. CONSEQUENTLY, THEY WAIT AND LET NATURE TAKE ITS COURSE. THESE MEN, WHOSE VERY EXISTENCE IS PERMEATED BY HORSES, SHARE A DEEP CONVICTION THAT THE ANIMALS MUST PRESERVE THEIR INSTINCT, REMAINING PARTIALLY WILD IN ORDER TO RETAIN THE GENETIC HERITAGE THAT HAS ENABLED THEM TO SURVIVE. THESE RIDERS OF THE PAMPAS DESPISE OUR CODDLED AND – IN THEIR VIEW – DEGENERATE RIDING-SCHOOL HORSES, AND I HAVE TO ADMIT THAT THEY MAY BE RIGHT.

THE BATTLE LASTS HALF AN HOUR, UNTIL THE CHALLENGER IS EXHAUSTED. THE YOUNG STALLION IS FORCED TO RETREAT, DISAPPOINTED AND WOUNDED IN BOTH BODY AND SOUL, AND RETURN TO HIS SOLITARY LIFE. HIS DREAM OF BECOMING THE HERD LEADER IS OVER, AT LEAST FOR THIS YEAR. HE MUST PREPARE HIMSELF AGAIN, AND SHOW HIMSELF TO BE STRONGER AND MORE COMBATIVE IF HE WISHES TO REPEAT THE CHALLENGE NEXT YEAR.

---

181   A fight between two Icelandic pony stallions beneath a stormy sky.

182 left and right   Stallions fighting for control over a herd of mares. These battles are merciless and can sometimes be fatal.

182 center   The winner of the fight can resume the leadership of the herd.

184   Two Spanish stallions, around three years old, play at fighting without roughness or anything real at stake, in a field near Ecija.

violence and fear

ALTHOUGH I FEEL ALMOST ASHAMED AND AM CONFUSED AND VISIBLY UPSET, I REALIZE THAT I DIDN'T MISS A SINGLE MOMENT OF THE SPECTACLE. WHAT SHOULD I MAKE OF THE SENSATIONS THAT I EXPERIENCED DURING THE DUEL? WHAT ARE THE REASONS BEHIND THIS AMBIGUOUS MIXTURE OF FASCINATION, EXCITEMENT AND FEAR? MY SOLE CERTAINTY IS THAT I'LL NEVER BE ABLE TO RIDE A STALLION AGAIN WITHOUT REMEMBERING THIS VIOLENT ENCOUNTER. IT GOES WITHOUT SAYING THAT MY ILLUSION OF CONTROL OVER A HORSE WOULDN'T LAST LONG IF FACED WITH ITS INNER STRENGTH AND LATENT FEROCITY – IF THE ANIMAL SHOULD CARE TO UNLEASH THEM.

COULD THE REASON FOR OUR FASCINATION WITH HORSES PERHAPS LIE IN THIS VIOLENCE AND UNTAMED POWER? MIGHT MAN HAVE BEEN CAPTURING WILD HORSES SINCE PREHISTORIC TIMES WITH THE AIM OF DOMINATING THIS DIABOLICAL AND TITANIC ENERGY? I THINK THAT IT IS SAFE TO SAY SO, FOR EARLY MAN WAS EVIDENTLY MESMERIZED BY HORSES. INDEED, THEY APPEAR IN SCULPTURES AND ROCK PAINTINGS FAR MORE FREQUENTLY THAN OTHER ANIMALS, SUCH AS MAMMOTHS OR BISON, WHOSE PHYSICAL STRENGTH WAS FAR GREATER.

RIGHT FROM THE VERY BEGINNING, RELATIONS BETWEEN MAN AND HORSES HAVE BEEN REGULATED BY VIOLENCE, NOT LEAST BECAUSE OF A SHARED HISTORY THAT COMMENCED WITH HUNTING. ONE HUNDRED THOUSAND YEARS AGO MAN TERRORIZED THE HERDS TO CORNER THEM, AND THE TRAPPED HORSES PREFERRED TO ALLOW THEMSELVES BE KILLED WITH SPEARS RATHER THAN BE DIVIDED.

THE DOMESTICATION OF THE HORSE ALSO ENTAILED VIOLENCE, FOR IT COMMENCED WITH THE CAPTURE OF YOUNG FOALS, OR RATHER WITH THE CAPTURE OF MARES IN FOAL. THE COLTS THAT WERE EXCESSIVELY AGGRESSIVE DURING ADOLESCENCE WERE SUBSEQUENTLY SLAUGHTERED FOR THEIR MEAT, WHILE THE FILLIES WERE USED AS BROOD MARES, TYING THEM TO A TREE WHEN IN SEASON TO BE COVERED BY WILD STALLIONS THAT NO MAN WOULD DARE TRY TO TAME.

WHY HAS MAN BEEN SO RELENTLESS IN HIS INTENT TO DOMESTICATE THE HORSE? WHY HAS HE TAKEN SO MANY RISKS AND STRUGGLED TO DOMINATE THE HORSE'S WILD STRENGTH AND UNPREDICTABLE CHARACTER? WHEN THE HORSE ENTERED THE GREAT FAMILY OF DOMESTIC ANIMALS, AROUND 3500 BC, MAN DID NOT NEED ANY MORE ANIMALS, FOR HE HAD ALREADY STARTED TO REAR COWS, SHEEP AND PIGS. OXEN PULLED THE PLOW AND OTHER ANIMALS SUPPLIED MEAT. THE HORSE IS NOT THE EASIEST OF THESE ANIMALS TO DOMESTICATE OR TO TRAIN. FURTHERMORE, MAN WAS NOT YET ABLE TO EXPLOIT ITS EXTRAORDINARY CAPACITIES TO THE FULL. IN ORDER TO TAKE ADVANTAGE OF THE HORSE'S SPEED AND STAMINA, IT WAS FIRST NECESSARY TO DEVELOP

RIDING, A TECHNIQUE THAT CALLS FOR COMPLEX EQUIPMENT: SADDLES AND BRIDLES. WE NOW KNOW THAT A MILLENNIUM OR MORE PASSED BETWEEN THE DOMESTICATION OF THE HORSE AND THE TIME IN WHICH IT WAS FIRST RIDDEN.

THE VIOLENCE THAT FASCINATED THE FIRST MEN IN THEIR DUELS WITH HORSES IS NOW MORE OF A MYTH THAN REALITY, AT LEAST IN THE LIFE OF TO-DAY'S PERFECTLY TRAINED STEEDS THAT ARE NO LONGER COMPELLED TO WOR-RY ABOUT THEIR SURVIVAL OR ENSURING THEIR DESCENT, FOR THEIR BREEDING IS NOW CODIFIED AND ORGANIZED BY MAN. WE KNOW THAT THE WILD HORSES OF THE PAST, LIKE THE PRZEWALSKI'S HORSE (STILL EXTANT IN VERY LIMITED NUMBERS IN TIBET AND MONGOLIA), WERE SKITTISH AND AGGRESSIVE ANIMALS, BUT ARABIANS AND OTHER PUREBREDS – SURROUNDED BY ATTENTIVE CARE FROM THEIR VERY FIRST DAYS – MERELY DESIRE A QUIET LIFE. ONLY TRUE STAL-LIONS MAY STILL DISPLAY GENUINELY VIOLENT BEHAVIOR, ESPECIALLY TO AS-SERT THEMSELVES AS PROCREATORS OVER THEIR COMPETITORS.

MAN IS EASILY INTIMIDATED BY THE THREAT OF A FLATTENED EAR, A MEN-ACING EYE OR THE SOUND OF TEETH BITING AT THE AIR, ESPECIALLY WHEN THE THREAT IS POSED BY AN ANIMAL WEIGHING CA. 900-1100 POUNDS (400-500 KG). THE VERY ESSENCE OF CIVILIZATION AIMS TO TEMPER THESE FORMS OF EXPRES-SION: WORDS HAVE REPLACED FAR MORE PERFUNCTORY EXPLANATIONS, SUCH AS A GRIMACE OR A GROWL, IN ORDER TO IMPOSE OUR RIGHT TO RESPECT OR

TRANQUILITY. CONSEQUENTLY, THE BODY LANGUAGE USED BY HORSES, DEVOID OF PRINCIPLES OR AFFECTED PHRASING, APPEARS FRIGHTENING TO CIVILIZED MAN. INDEED, MAN INTERPRETS IT AS A PERSONAL FORM OF AGGRESSION, WHEREAS HORSES ARE SIMPLY STATING THE LIMITS, AND HOW MUCH THEY IN-TEND TO ACCEPT.

THE MORE I LIVE WITH HORSES, THE MORE I REALIZE THAT WHAT IS OFTEN PERCEIVED AS VIOLENCE AND AGGRESSION IS SIMPLY A FORM OF LANGUAGE. THIS IS THE CASE OF THE DOMINANT MARE WHO FLATTENS HER EARS TO WARD OFF ANOTHER WHO HAS COME TOO CLOSE, THE BROOD MARE WHO NIPS HER FOAL BECAUSE HE HAS OVERSTEPPED THE BOUNDS, OR THE STALLION WHO SEEMS TO CHARGE ANOTHER MEMBER OF THE HERD. AT FIRST SIGHT, WHILE DIS-PLAYS OF AGGRESSION WITHIN A GROUP MAY NOT APPEAR TO BE PARTICULAR-LY NUMEROUS, THEY DO SEEM TO BE A REGULAR OCCURRENCE. HOWEVER, IF WE PLAY THEM DOWN AND VIEW THEM WITHOUT PRECONCEPTIONS, A NEW INTER-PRETATION IS POSSIBLE. THIS BODY LANGUAGE IS ACTUALLY USED TO IMPLE-MENT A PRECISE, UNCHANGEABLE SOCIAL CODE, WHICH ENSURES PEACE AND HARMONY AMONG THE HERD. HORSES REACT IMMEDIATELY TO THESE VISUAL CODES (FLATTENED EARS, SWISHING TAILS, OR SWAYING HEADS) IN ORDER TO FACE OR AVOID CONFRONTATION. CONSEQUENTLY, THREATS ARE FREQUENT OCCURRENCES, BUT CLASHES ARE VERY RARE AND EACH ANIMAL STAYS IN ITS

186-187   This foal, frightened by my presence, takes refuge next to his mother. Young males sometimes behave very protectively toward their mothers, and almost all of them try to mount her, for the instinct of the future stallion is already very strong.

189   Rivalry between two siblings: the arrival of the spring and the estrus of the mares produce a rush of hormones.

PLACE WITHOUT THREATENING THE UNITY OF THE GROUP.

ACTUALLY HORSES ARE EXEMPLARILY PACIFIC ANIMALS THAT PAINSTAKINGLY AVOID CONFLICT AND DISPLAY GREAT SOLIDARITY. THE REASON FOR THIS BEHAVIOR IS SIMPLE: THREATS AND HAZARDS ARE EXTERNAL FACTORS. BY LIVING IN A HERD AND MAINTAINING FRIENDLY GROUP RELATIONS, HORSES ARE ABLE TO FACE TRUE THREATS, SUCH AS PREDATORS CROUCHING IN THE BUSHES, READY TO SPRING A SURPRISE ATTACK. THEIR BRETHREN ARE NEITHER COMPETITORS NOR ENEMIES, BUT COULD SAVE THE LIVES OF THE OTHER MEMBERS OF THE HERD, BY RAISING THE ALARM, FOR EXAMPLE. THIS PRINCIPLE MAY SEEM TOTALLY OUTDATED TODAY, FOR MOST HORSES HAVE NOT EXPERIENCED THE THREAT OF PREDATORS FOR HUNDREDS OF GENERATIONS. HOWEVER, FEAR REMAINS A VISCERAL SENTIMENT.

THE MODERN HORSE ALWAYS ACTS AS A POTENTIAL PREY AND A VULNERABLE BEING IN RESPECT TO THE OUTSIDE WORLD. THE SAME HORSE THAT ACTS AS A PROUD CHAMPION IN THE RING IS TERRIFIED BY THE RUSTLING OF A BUSH, THE PRESENCE OF AN UNUSUAL OBJECT OR THE NOISE OF AN ENGINE. HIS FEAR IS BOUNDLESS, SINCERE AND TOTAL; HIS HEART SEEMS TO BEAT SO HARD AS TO EXPLODE, HIS POPPING EYES DESPERATELY SEEK TO SEE THE SOURCE OF THE DANGER, AND HIS ENTIRE BODY SHAKES AND TREMBLES, READY TO BOLT. AT TIMES HORSES MAY DISPLAY HINTS OF VIOLENCE, WHICH IS SOMETIMES SIMU-

violence and fear

LATED, BUT THEIR FEAR IS ALWAYS DEEPLY ROOTED, EASILY TRIGGERED AND READY TO POSSESS THEM COMPLETELY. THREATENING BEHAVIOR HAS LED TO IMAGE OF THE HORSE AS A VIOLENT ANIMAL, WHILE ITS FEARS HAVE MADE PEOPLE CONSIDER IT STUPID. HOWEVER, THIS ONCE AGAIN LEADS US TO UNDERESTIMATE THE TRUE NATURE OF THIS MAGNIFICENT ANIMAL. THROUGHOUT THEIR 60 MILLION YEARS OF THEIR EVOLUTION, HORSES HAVE ALWAYS BEEN PREY. WHEN FACED WITH PREDATORS, THEY COULD HAVE TRIED TO DEFEND THEMSELVES BRAVELY WITH THEIR TEETH AND, PARTICULARLY, WITH THEIR HOOVES, BUT THEIR ATTACKERS USUALLY HAD LETHAL WEAPONS, SUCH AS CLAWS OR TUSKS, AND OFTEN A PACK STRATEGY THAT LEFT THE HORSES WITH LITTLE CHANCE OF ESCAPE. FLEEING WAS THEIR ONLY GUARANTEE OF SAFETY, AS LONG AS THEY DID SO AS FAST AS POSSIBLE. IMAGINE MILLIONS OF GENERATIONS OF HORSES BEING DEVOURED AND ONLY A FEW DOZEN SURVIVING TO ENJOY AN EXISTENCE OUT OF REACH OF THESE TRAGEDIES. FORTUNATELY THE SURVIVAL INSTINCT IS NOT EASILY CHANGED.

THROUGHOUT MOST OF THE WORLD MAN – WHO HAS NOT BEEN DEVOURED FOR THOUSANDS OF YEARS – CONTINUES TO RELIVE HIS ANCESTRAL FEARS IN THE FORM OF TERRIBLE NIGHTMARES IN WHICH HE IS HUNTED BY WOLVES, ALIENS AND OGRES THAT ARE READY TO PREY ON HIM. VERY FEW PEOPLE ARE CAPABLE OF CROSSING A FOREST ALONE AT NIGHT OR SLEEPING IN THE WILD, EVEN THOUGH THEY WOULD BE NOT BE RUNNING ANY RISK AT ALL, FOR THEY CERTAINLY WOULD NOT BE DEVOURED BY WILD ANIMALS. ARE THEY STUPID? NO, THEY TOO ARE EXPRESSING THE FEARS THAT HAVE PERSECUTED THEIR SPECIES OVER THE CENTURIES.

UNDERSTANDING THE HORSE'S VISCERAL FEAR ALSO ENTAILS BEING AWARE OF A GREAT DIFFERENCE BETWEEN HORSE AND MAN AND PREY AND PREDATOR: MAN DEFENDS HIMSELF BY FACING DANGER IN ORDER TO ASSESS IT, WHILE THE HORSE DEFENDS ITSELF BY FLEEING AS FAST AS POSSIBLE AND THEN EXAMINING THE SITUATION FROM A DISTANCE. THE ONLY THING THAT CAN TEMPER ITS FEARFUL NATURE IS FEELING PROTECTED. IF A HORSE BELIEVES THAT YOU ARE CAPABLE OF FACING THE DANGER, SAVING HIM FROM A DIFFICULT SITUATION AND FINDING SOLUTIONS TO PROBLEMS, HE WILL MANAGE TO OVERCOME MANY OF HIS FEARS AND GRADUALLY RECOVER HIS CALM AND CONFIDENCE. IT MAY TAKE YEARS BEFORE A HORSE WILL CONSIDER YOU WORTHY OF HIS TRUST AND FOLLOW YOU TO THE ENDS OF THE EARTH WITHOUT THE SLIGHTEST HESITATION. HOWEVER, WHEN HE DOES HE WILL PUT HIS LIFE IN YOUR HANDS, AND IT IS UP TO YOU TO BE EQUAL TO THIS GREAT RESPONSIBILITY. THIS MUTUAL TRUST IS A STRANGE MORAL CONTRACT BETWEEN A PREDATOR AND ITS ANCIENT PREY, A MAN AWED BY THE VIOLENCE OF THE HORSE AND AN ANIMAL FRIGHTENED BY ANYTHING THAT MOVES. BUT ARE NOT THE NOBLEST CONQUESTS ALSO THE MOST SURPRISING ONES? WE MAY ASK OURSELVES WHETHER IT WAS THE HORSE'S VIOLENCE OR VULNERABILITY THAT DEFINITIVELY SEDUCED MAN. BOTH OF THESE ASPECTS WERE UNDOUBTEDLY CRUCIAL: THE HORSE'S VIOLENT SIDE REMINDS US OF WHAT WE ARE TRYING TO SUPPRESS AND CODIFY – IN A CIVILIZING EFFORT THAT CONSTANTLY THREATENS TO REGRESS – WHILE THE VULNERABILITY OF THIS POWERFUL AND NOBLE ANIMAL TAKES US BACK TO OUR OWN VISCERAL FEARS AND THE FRAGILITY OF OUR LIVES AND OUR CERTAINTIES AND DEFENSES, WHICH CAN OFTEN BE SWEPT AWAY IN A FRACTION OF A SECOND.

190 and 190-191 The young bay male is attempting to oust the two-colored stallion, confronting him in a fierce battle that may last hours. One of the fighters may withdraw while still in a fit state, but if the stallions persist, they may cause each other serious wounds that can prove fatal. The mares stand back and watch the fight, whose outcome will directly affect their future as breeding stock. The gauchos who own the horses allow them to fight, entrusting natural selection to determine which is the best stallion.

192-193 The onlooker is dazed by such a rough and violent
battle, remaining powerless on the vibrating ground as the
horses lash out with their hooves, and listening to the
terrifying and deafening sound of bodies clashing and the
rasping breath of the gasping fighters. Frightened, fascinated
and astounded, the memory of this strange sensation of total
and brutal ferocity will endure long after the fight.

194-195 and 195   The old two-colored stallion uses his great experience and intelligence to beat the intruder out of the group, without either of the horses suffering too much damage. He will be able to mount the mares again this year, thus ensuring his progeny.

violence and fear

196-197   Becoming and remaining the stallion of a herd of mares is hard work, because the role is continuously disputed. When in heat, the females may be tempted by the single males that orbit around the herd, or their stallion may simply be dispossessed by a younger or stronger horse.

violence and fear

198 and 199   Around 100 colts aged between two and three years old are herded together in the mountain pastures of Kufstein, between Austria and Germany, where they spend 6 months a year on the steep slopes at altitudes between 650 and 8200 feet. In normal conditions, without the presence of mares, the group is entirely pacific. The horses sometimes play virile games, but without any true aggressiveness – except this morning, when two young males have decided to fight.

200 and 201   The Friesian stallion Legolas and his son Aramis settle scores: the youngster must show his father respect, yet reveals that he is still tempted to affirm his new strength. However, their honor is safe, for both defer to their respective roles. Their displays immediately remind me of the beautiful and dramatic paintings of horses displayed at the Prado or in the Louvre.

202 and 203   Two young Spanish stallions seem to be dancing in an embrace. This kind of "waltz" is a game played by young males to learn how to fight. Nothing in particular is at stake, nor is there any goal other than to demonstrate one's tactics and physical strength, in order to be capable of dealing with a true rival one day.

204 and 205   During a fight, horses use their hooves, striking their adversary like a boxer; their teeth, to bite deeply; and the weight of their entire body, which they raise and let drop on their rival to knock him off balance.

206   A fight between Haflingers in the Italian Tyrol, where breeders release the young males in the boundless mountain pastures each spring. The horses fight on the first day in order to establish the hierarchy within the herd. Each individual subsequently respects its status and the group becomes peaceful again.

207   It is no easy task trying to pacify two dominant males that provoke each other, and care must be taken to avoid any stray bites that may come one's way!

208 and 209   The flying manes of a couple of Gypsy Vanners, which resemble a pair of squabbling goddesses! Even this very brave and peaceful breed is capable of changing tone when one of the members of the group becomes overly provocative.

violence and fear

210-211   This horse not only flattens its ears as a threatening gesture, but also to protect them from bites, and an expression of hate is clearly visible in its eyes.

212 and 213   An outbreak of anger between two Friesians on the bright and cold snow of a winter morning. Following the first fierce blows, their breathing becomes heavier, their movements slower and their animosity is appeased. The sweat-soaked horses, steaming in the icy air, eventually decide not to take things any further.

214-215   Those who do not gallop fast enough lose the protection of the herd, and so all the members run like the wind. Young horses like these greatly fear being isolated and separated from the herd. At the age of just a year, newly separated from their mothers, they are still inexperienced and very vulnerable.

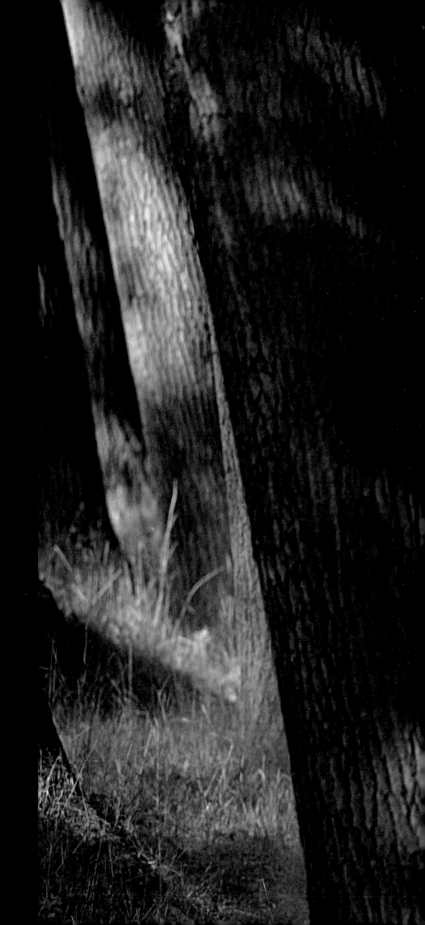

violence and fear

216-217   Forests are always hostile and unpredictable environments for wild horses,
which are unable to see well when surrounded by trees and consequently risk falling
easy prey to predators. They must thus cross woods as quickly as possible.

violence and fear

218-219   The herd and flight represent the only hopes of
survival for a horse in danger. We always tend to
underestimate or misunderstand the horse's visceral fear. Ever
since it was domesticated, over 5000 years ago, it has been
safe from predators, yet it continues to shy and flee at the
tiniest suspicious noise. However, before being domesticated,
no less than 60 million years conditioned it to consider flight
the best form of survival for the species.

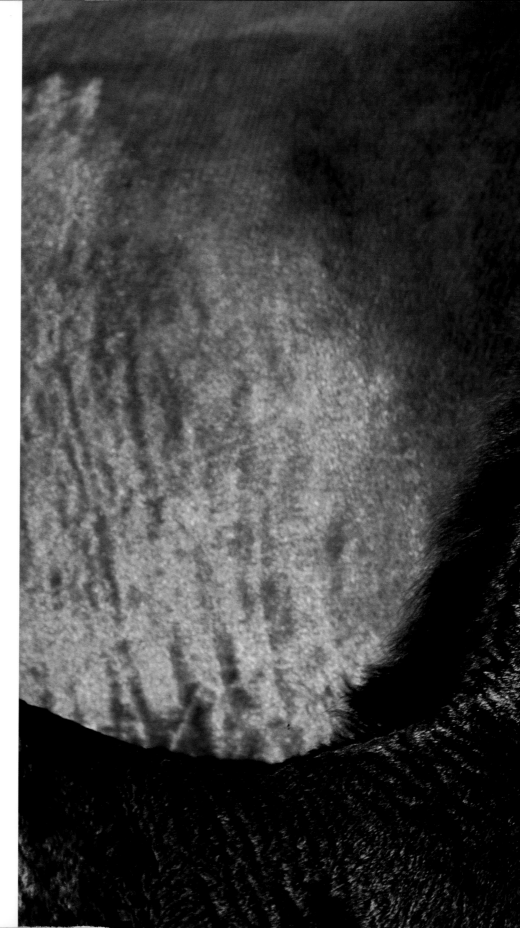

220-221   This Friesian foal takes refuge next to its mother, who is ready to face any danger to protect her offspring. Indeed, as pregnancy progresses, the mare becomes increasingly diffident and detached, even toward other horses. During birth, she protects her foal against intruders and keeps it alongside her for a whole month. In turn, whenever the foal is frightened, it spontaneously takes refuge alongside her. It is not until the end of adolescence, toward the age of one and a half, that it is driven out from the group and its mother in order to live as an adult.

222 and 222-223   Horses' eyes betray their emotions, and you can be sure that they are uneasy when they open them wide, revealing the white that surrounds the iris. Another characteristic pose is represented by a high head carriage with dilated nostrils and raised tail, indicating that the horse is on the alert. However, as soon as it understands what's going on and feels reassured, the tension may disappear as fast as it came.

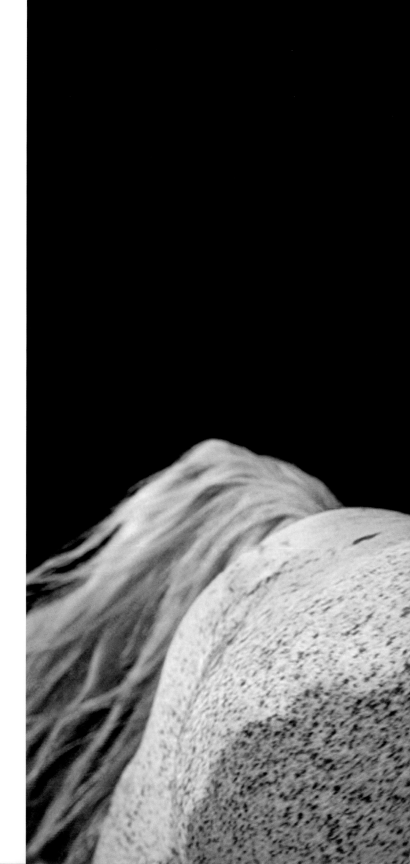

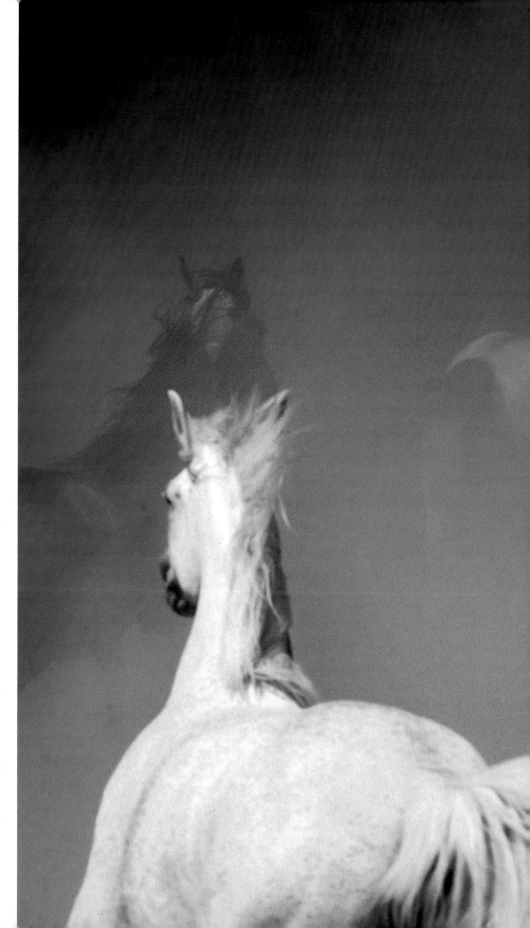

224-225   A group of Arabian brood mares of the Al Badia *haras* of Cairo gallop across the Egyptian desert. These fluid, airy and delicate "Drinkers of the Wind" have inspired countless legends, entire collections of poetry, and numerous verses of the Koran.

226-227   A group of 500-1000 horses moves across the pampas, forming waves similar to those created by the wind in long grass, as the sea of bodies flows to the deafening sound of hooves. They live here, in a semi-wild state, thus preserving their legendary instinct and stamina. For these horses, man is a danger, against which they fight strenuously when captured. While brutal breaking will force them to submit, and habit will calm them, their instinct will never abandon them.

sensitivity and fragility

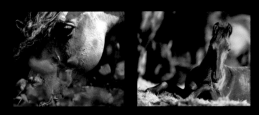

sensitivity and fragility

HE'S JUST EMERGED FROM HIS MOTHER'S WARM BODY AND IS SOAKING WET WITH MATTED HAIR, AND A LITTLE DAZED AND

BEWILDERED IN THE NEW WORLD THAT HE'S GRADUALLY DISCOVERING. THE FOAL REMAINS LYING FOR A FEW MINUTES, LEGS

SPLAYED, AS HE RECOVERS HIS STRENGTH FOLLOWING BIRTH. HE ALREADY HOLDS UP HIS HEAD, SMELLING THE WARM STRAW AND

HIS MOTHER, WHO CONTINUES TO LICK HIM. THEN, OFTEN IN THE SPACE OF LESS THAN AN HOUR, HE'S ALREADY TRYING TO

STAND UP ON HIS LONG LEGS. HE CLUMSILY PUSHES HIS HINDQUARTERS UPWARDS, BUT CANNOT YET RAISE HIS SHOULDERS. THEN

HE CHANGES STRATEGY AND TRIES TO PULL HIMSELF ONTO HIS FRONT LEGS. WHEN HE FINALLY MANAGES TO COORDINATE HIS

MOVEMENTS AND HAUL HIMSELF UP ONTO HIS LONG SLENDER LEGS, HE TOPPLES OVER AND COLLAPSES ON THE STRAW. AFTER

A FEW UNSUCCESSFUL ATTEMPTS, HE FINALLY MANAGES TO KEEP HIS BALANCE ON HIS SPLAYED AND TREMBLING LEGS, AND WILL

SOON TAKE HIS FIRST STEPS. IT SEEMS AS THOUGH AN INVISIBLE FORCE IS TELLING HIM TO HURRY, AND THIS IRREPRESSIBLE IN-

STINCT DRIVES HIM TO PERSEVERE, HOWEVER GREAT THE EFFORT.

THIS TOUCHING SPECTACLE MERELY MARKS THE START OF THE STRUGGLE FOR LIFE. THE HORSE'S UNBOUNDED STRENGTH RE-

SIDES IN THIS ENERGY THAT DRIVES IT TO WALK AND MOVE AS SOON AS IT LEAVES THE SAFETY OF ITS MOTHER'S WOMB. HOW-

EVER, THIS STRENGTH HIDES AN EQUALLY GREAT WEAKNESS, WHICH REPRESENTS A MORTAL RISK: IF THE FOAL DOESN'T MANAGE

TO HAUL HIMSELF TO HIS FEET DURING THE VERY FIRST HOURS OF LIFE, HE IS DOOMED, FOR HE NEEDS TO REACH HIS MOTHER'S

UDDER TO DRINK THE RICH COLOSTRUM (MILK CONTAINING A NATURAL LAXATIVE) THAT WILL PROTECT HIM AND GIVE HIM THE

NECESSARY ENERGY TO SURVIVE. IF HE DOES NOT MANAGE TO DO SO DURING THE FIRST SIX HOURS, HIS LIFE WILL BE IN PERIL. IN

NATURE, WITHOUT HUMAN INTERVENTION, THE FOAL GROWS WEAKER BY THE HOUR AND CAN DIE IF HE DOESN'T SUCKLE IN TIME.

NOT MOVING AND REMAINING LYING DOWN MEANS CERTAIN DEATH, AT THE BEGINNING AS AT THE END OF LIFE. OLD HORSES GROW WEAKER VERY GRADUALLY, LIMITING THEIR MOVEMENTS AND LYING DOWN EVER MORE RARELY IN ORDER TO AVOID THE FATAL RISK OF NOT BEING ABLE TO GET UP AGAIN. LIKE A FOAL UNABLE TO GATHER THE STRENGTH TO STAND UP, THE OLD HORSE CAN NO LONGER FIND THE ENERGY TO CLIMB TO HIS FEET AND EXHAUSTS HIMSELF BY TRYING AND RETRYING TO PERFORM A MOVEMENT THAT HE HAS MADE THOUSANDS OF TIMES. HOWEVER, HE IS UNABLE TO MANAGE IT AND HIS STRENGTH ABANDONS HIM. HE MERELY RAISES HIS HEAD EVERY NOW AND THEN WITH A SIGH, BEFORE GIVING UP HIS ATTEMPTS AND AWAITING DEATH. THE GREAT COMPLEXITY OF THE HORSE IS VERY EVIDENT IN THIS MOMENT: HIS ENORMOUS STRENGTH AND PRESENT INSTINCT MUST COMPENSATE AN INFINITE FRAGILITY. IT IS HARD TO CONSTRUE HOW SUCH A GREAT AND POWERFUL ANIMAL CAN BE SO DELICATE. THE SLIGHTEST CHANGE IN HIS DIET REPRESENTS A SERIOUS THREAT TO HIS HEALTH, FOR HE COULD DIE OF COLIC IN THE SPACE OF A FEW HOURS. FURTHERMORE, IF HE PUTS ON WEIGHT HE RISKS FOOT ROT; IF HE BREAKS A LEG HE IS CONDEMNED (AND EVERY NOW AND THEN IT CAN HAPPEN AT THE GALLOP, WITH A LOUD NOISE OF CRACKING BONE); WHILE THE KICK OF ANOTHER HORSE, WITHOUT EXCESSIVE VIOLENCE, COULD RUIN HIM FOREVER. COUNTLESS HORSES THAT ARE CONSIDERED STRAIGHTFORWARD AND PROBLEM-FREE BECOME DESOLATE WHEN THEIR EQUILIBRIUM IS UPSET. A CHANGE OF OWNER, STABLE OR FIELD MATE IS ALL THAT IT TAKES TO MAKE THEIR LIVES A MISERY, EVEN IF THE CHANGE WAS MOTIVATED BY THE BEST INTENTIONS.

229   The eyes of this huge and powerful Friesian are bottomless pools of gentleness.

230 left   A purebred Arabian on the alert.

230 center   A Trakhener foal discovering the world.

230 right   An Arabian foal has taken refuge next to his mother.

231   The first exchange of effusions just a few minutes after birth.

sensitivity and fragility

sensitivity and fragility

I REMEMBER LENDING MY HORSE TO ANOTHER RIDER ONCE DURING A PERIOD IN WHICH I COULD NOT VISIT HIM AS OFTEN AS HE WAS ACCUSTOMED. I THOUGHT THAT HIS PHYSICAL AND MENTAL EQUILIBRIUM WERE SOUND ENOUGH TO ALLOW HIM TO BENEFIT FROM THE COMPANY OF THIS STRANGER, WHOSE RIDING SKILLS AND HABITS I'D CAREFULLY OBSERVED. IN THE SPACE OF JUST THREE MONTHS, MARKED BY TWO SHORT WEEKLY SESSIONS IN THE COMPANY OF THE YOUNG WOMAN, MY HANDSOME FRIEND, WHOM I'D CONSIDERED IMPERTURBABLE, UNDERWENT A DRAMATIC TRANSFORMATION. HE LOST A GREAT DEAL OF WEIGHT, CAUSING HIS BACK TO SAG LIKE THAT OF A HORSE FIVE OR TEN YEARS OLDER, BECAME UNCONTROLLABLE TO RIDE AND EVEN STARTED JIBBING. THIS CHANGE WAS INCREDIBLE AND, ABOVE ALL, COMPLETELY OUT OF PROPORTION IN RESPECT TO WHAT I HAD OBSERVED DURING THE SESSIONS WITH HIS OCCASIONAL RIDER. I HAD TO HALT THOSE APPARENTLY INNOCENT ENCOUNTERS AND SUBSEQUENTLY WAIT SIX MONTHS BEFORE MY DEAR COMPANION RETURNED TO HIS OLD SELF. THE HORSE THAT I HAD KNOWN FOR TEN YEARS AND HAD NEVER EVEN IMAGINED COULD CHANGE, HAD BECOME A COMPLETELY DIFFERENT ANIMAL IN THE SPACE OF JUST A FEW WEEKS.

THE HYPERSENSITIVITY OF HORSES IS ALWAYS CLEAR TO SEE. IT'S AS THOUGH THEY LIVE THEIR DAILY LIVES WITH FAR GREATER INTENSITY THAN MAN. THEIR PERCEPTION OF FLAVORS, SMELLS AND SOUNDS IS INCONCEIVABLE TO OUR SENSES.

IF THE WATER IS SLIGHTLY CHLORINATED, THEN HORSES ARE DISGUSTED, AND THEY CHOOSE WHICH GRASS TO EAT PLANT BY PLANT, SPITTING OUT EACH BLADE THAT IS NOT TO THEIR LIKING. THEY ARE ABLE TO RECOGNIZE WHICH PLANTS THEY GRAZED YEARS EARLIER IN THE FIELDS WHERE THEY SPENT THEIR YOUTH, AND IMMEDIATELY TELL THE POISONOUS ONES HIDDEN IN THE MIDST OF THE OTHERS. THEY CAN ESTABLISH THE SEX, AGE AND HORMONAL STATE OF OTHER HORSES WITHOUT EVEN SEEING THEM, MERELY FROM THEIR DROPPINGS. THEIR SENSE OF TOUCH IS ALSO IMPRESSIVE, FOR THEY ARE DISTURBED BY A FLY OR A LEAF ON THEIR BACKS, AND WILL SHAKE IT OFF IMMEDIATELY. ALTHOUGH THEY HAVE NO HANDS, THEIR NOSES AND SURROUNDING WHISKERS ALLOW THEM AN EXTRAORDINARY SENSITIVITY TO OBJECTS AND TEMPERATURES. THEY TOUCH EVERYTHING THAT THEY DISCOVER, NUDGING IT WITH THEIR LIPS TO ASSURE THEMSELVES OF ITS HARMLESSNESS. THEY HAVE INCREDIBLE MEMORIES AND KNOW EVERY SINGLE DETAIL OF THEIR ENVIRONMENT, EACH SLOPE AND BUSH THAT THEY ENCOUNTER DURING THEIR REGULAR RIDES. IF JUST ONE THING IS MISSING FROM THEIR ENVIRONMENT, THEY ARE ON THE ALERT, SURPRISED AND EVEN UNEASY. THE SIGHT OF A FALLEN TREE OR A CLOSED DOOR THAT IS NORMALLY OPEN IS ENOUGH TO ALARM THEM. IF YOU FOLLOW THE SAME ROUTE AGAIN, EVEN A MONTH LATER, THE HORSE WILL DISPLAY HIS NERVOUSNESS AS SOON AS YOU APPROACH THAT AREA. HE REFLECTS AND ATTRIBUTES CRUCIAL

IMPORTANCE TO WHAT WILL HAPPEN THIS TIME, SEEMING TO ASK HIMSELF WHETHER EVERYTHING IS BACK TO NORMAL. DESPITE THE AIR OF AN IMPASSIVE HERBIVORE THAT SPENDS THREE-QUARTERS OF ITS LIFE WITH ITS NOSE IN THE GRASS, THE HORSE EXPERIENCES EVERY SINGLE MOMENT AND EVERY LITTLE THING WITH AN INTENSITY THAT IS BEYOND OUR COMPREHENSION. HE OBSERVES THE SLIGHTEST MOVEMENT AND EVERY CHANGE OF POSITION, ALWAYS AWARE OF WHERE YOU ARE AND WHAT YOU'RE DOING. IT'S ACTUALLY VERY EASY FOR HIM, AS HE DOESN'T EVEN NEED TO TURN HIS HEAD TO SEE YOU. INDEED HIS 350-DEGREE VISION ENSURES INFALLIBLE MONITORING, WHICH IS FAR MORE EFFICIENT THAN THE MOST SOPHISTICATED VIDEO-SURVEILLANCE SYSTEMS. IF YOU HAPPEN TO CHANGE EVEN THE SLIGHTEST DETAIL OF YOUR DAILY ROUTINE, THIS TRANQUIL HERBIVORE SUDDENLY BECOMES ALERT AND UNEASY, AS HE TRIES TO COMPREHEND THE NEW SITUATION. THIS SILENT FRIEND AND ANGELIC BEING THAT SEES ALL KNOWS EVERYTHING ABOUT YOU: WHETHER YOU'RE WEARING A NEW JACKET, HAVE CHANGED PERFUME OR HAVE BETRAYED HIM WITH ANOTHER HORSE FOR SECRET RIDES. MORE SURPRISING STILL IS HIS INFALLIBLE ABILITY TO UNDERSTAND YOUR MENTAL STATE. IF YOU ARRIVE AT THE STABLES AFTER AN HOUR STUCK IN THE TRAFFIC OR FOLLOWING A HEATED DISCUSSION, YOUR COMPANION WILL BECOME TENSE AS SOON AS HE SEES YOU. HE'S A TRUE EMOTIONAL SPONGE, WHO ABSORBS YOUR ANGER AND IRRITATION, AND YOU CAN BE SURE THAT HE WON'T DO ANYTHING TO PLEASE YOU THAT DAY, FOR HE WILL BE TENSE, DISTRACTED AND OBSTINATE – IN SHORT, YOUR MIRROR IMAGE! THIS NEVER FAILS TO EXASPERATE THE RIDER WHO WENT TO THE STABLES TO RELAX, BUT THIS HYPERSENSITIVE ANIMAL DEMANDS THAT WE ABANDON OUR ANGER BEFORE MOUNTING HIM, AND PURIFY OURSELVES IN ORDER TO ENJOY THE HEAVENLY EXPERIENCE OF THE SADDLE. RIDING IS THUS AN ART OF LIVING AND AN ETERNAL PHILOSOPHY LESSON. IF YOU ARRIVE IN A LIGHTHEARTED, WILLING AND KIND MOOD, YOU'LL FIND AN IDEAL PARTNER. IF YOU'RE SAD OR DISCOURAGED, HE'LL BLOW ON YOUR NECK, REST HIS HEAD ON YOUR SHOULDER AND STAY CLOSE TO YOU, SEEMING TO SAY, "DON'T WORRY, I'M HERE." HE'S A GOOD LISTENER AND WILL SYMPATHETICALLY WATCH YOU CRY, CARESSING YOUR CHEEKS WITH HIS DELICATE LIPS, AS THOUGH DRYING YOUR TEARS.

THE SENSITIVITY AND DELICACY OF HORSES ARE SO PRONOUNCED THAT THEY ARE NOW USED AS PSYCHOTHERAPISTS, TO SOOTHE MENTAL PAIN AND TO TREAT PHYSICAL DISABILITIES. THE MOVEMENT WAS BORN IN EUROPE DURING THE 1970S AND SUBSEQUENTLY REACHED THE UNITED STATES. ENLIGHTENED HORSE LOVERS, CONVINCED OF THE EMPATHIC ABILITY AND GREAT THERAPEUTIC POTENTIAL OF THESE ANIMALS, LAUNCHED A SERIES OF ENCOUNTERS WITH PEOPLE WITH MULTIPLE HANDICAPS. THE RESULTS WERE SURPRISING, AND SO EVIDENT THAT HIPPOTHERAPY NOW ENJOYS UNIVERSAL RECOGNITION. THE GREAT-

EST SUCCESS WAS OBTAINED WITH MALTREATED OR AUTISTIC CHILDREN: WOUNDED CREATURES WHO NO LONGER SPOKE TO ADULTS AND HAD CLOSED THEMSELVES IN THEIR OWN INNER WORLD, REFUSING ALL FORMS OF COMMUNICATION, SOMETIMES FOR YEARS. HOWEVER, CONTACT WITH HORSES ENABLED THEM TO RETURN MIRACULOUSLY TO LIFE IN THE SPACE OF JUST A FEW MONTHS. EVEN THOSE WHO LIMIT THEIR CONTACT WITH THE ANIMALS AND DO NOT RIDE THEM HAVE BEEN SEEN TO BENEFIT FROM THESE POSITIVE RESULTS. THERE ARE MANY, COMPLEX REASONS FOR THIS SUCCESS. THE BOND BETWEEN INVALIDS AND HORSES IS ESTABLISHED AT DIFFERENT LEVELS, WITH DIFFERENT PROCEDURES. FIRST OF ALL, IT TAKES PLACE THROUGH THE BODY WITH THE GENTLE, WARM AND DELICATE PHYSICAL CONTACT CREATED BY THE REGULAR SWAYING OF RIDING AT A STEADY PACE. BUT THERE IS ALSO THE PSYCHOLOGICAL ASPECT, IN WHICH OUR FOUR-LEGGED THERAPISTS EXCEL. INDEED, HORSES IMMEDIATELY SENSE WHEN THEY ARE DEALING WITH AN UNHAPPY, WITHDRAWN AND FRIGHTENED CREATURE, WHOM THEY WILL APPROACH DELICATELY, AS THOUGH ATTRACTED BY A CALAMITY. IT'S AS THOUGH THE PERSON WHO IS AFRAID TO ESTABLISH CONTACT WITH THE ANIMAL STIMULATES IT TO PROVOKE HIM. THE HORSE WILL THUS BRUSH THE PERSON'S HAND WITH ITS LIPS, SMELL HIS NECK AND NIP HIS SLEEVE, BUT SO SHYLY AND DELICATELY THAT IS IMPOSSIBLE TO FEEL THREATENED. THE HORSE MAKES CONTACT, BUT AT THE SAME TIME SHOWS

sensitivity and fragility

THAT IT IS READY TO TAKE FLIGHT AND IS FRAGILE AND SENSITIVE TO THE SLIGHTEST MOVEMENT. THE HORSE'S FRAGILITY AND SENSITIVITY ENABLE CONTACT TO BE ESTABLISHED. THIS LARGE AND POWERFUL ANIMAL HAS SHOWN INTEREST IN A SMALL DEFENSELESS CREATURE AND SHOWS ITSELF WILLING AND ATTENTIVE TO ALL KINDS OF INTERACTION, TO WHICH IT RESPONDS IN ITS OWN WAY, ASKING NOTHING AND WITHOUT EVER JUDGING OR ASSESSING. HORSES ARE INFINITELY PATIENT AND DO NOT EXPECT RESULTS; THEY HAVE NO HIDDEN AGENDA AND ARE CAPABLE OF ENJOYING THE PRESENCE OF THE OTHER, REMAINING TOGETHER IN TENDER INTIMACY. IN THE PRESENCE OF A HORSE WE FEEL ENVELOPED BY THE HEAT OF ITS LARGE BODY, THE SOFTNESS OF ITS COAT, THE CALMNESS OF ITS DEEP BREATHING AND SIGHS, THE SLOW RHYTHM OF ITS CHEWING AND THE DELICACY OF ITS MOVEMENTS. OUR DEFENSES ARE LOWERED, OUR HEARTS APPEASED AND OUR SPIRITS FREED. AFTER A FEW MINUTES OF LOOKING AT THE ANIMAL AND LISTENING TO IT IN THE INTIMATE SETTING OF ITS LOOSE BOX WE EXPERIENCE A STATE OF GRACE, PRAYER AND MEDITATION. TRANQUILITY RETURNS TO OUR MOST HIDDEN SELVES AND OUR INNER FORCE CAN ONCE AGAIN OCCUPY ITS SPACE, LIKE A WATERCOURSE WHOSE FLOODGATES HAVE SUDDENLY BEEN OPENED. THE FLOW REDISCOVERS ITS RIVERBEDS AND CHANNELS, REACHING EVEN THE MOST SECRET RECESSES OF OUR BODIES. SOME SAY THAT THE AURA AND ENERGY OF HORSES ARE SO IMMENSE AND POWERFUL THAT THOSE WHO COME INTO CONTACT WITH THEM ARE ABLE TO RECOVER AND REPLENISH THEIR OWN STORE OF ENERGY, AND I AM SURE THAT THIS IS TRUE. AT LEAST THIS IS WHAT I HAVE ALWAYS SENSED, ALTHOUGH I AM NOT NECESSARILY ABLE TO EXPLAIN IT. ALTHOUGH THEIR MERE PRESENCE HAS A HEALING EFFECT, WE MUST NOT CONSIDER HORSES PASSIVE FIGURES IN OUR RECOVERY FROM AILMENTS GREAT OR SMALL. INDEED, THEY INTERACT AND PLAY A TRUE THERAPEUTIC ROLE IN THE RELATIONSHIP WITH THE SICK. THEY APPROACH CERTAIN PEOPLE OF THEIR OWN ACCORD, TOUCHING PARTICULAR PARTS OF THEIR BODIES AND MASSAGING THEM WITH THEIR LIPS. THESE POINTS UNFAILINGLY CORRESPOND TO THE SITE OF THE TENSION, TRAUMA OR EVEN ACTUAL DISEASES, SUCH AS ULCERS OR CANCER. I WAS UNABLE TO BELIEVE THE STORIES OF THE HORSE'S ROLE IN PSYCHOTHERAPY SESSIONS AND THUS SOMEWHAT DEFIANTLY ENROLLED ON A COURSE HELD BY LINDA KOHANOV, THE AUTHOR OF THE BOOK ENTITLED *THE TAO OF EQUUS*. DURING THOSE FEW DAYS I WITNESSED INCREDIBLE SESSIONS, IN WHICH HER BLACK STALLION ACHIEVED THE IMPOSSIBLE. HE MANAGED TO ADAPT TO THE DIFFERENT PEOPLE WITH WHOM HE WAS FACED, ADDRESSING THEM IN A PARTICULAR MANNER AND EACH TIME HE MANAGED TO TOUCH THEIR SENSITIVE SPOT, WHETHER MENTAL OR PHYSICAL. HE ADMINISTERED TENDERNESS, HUMOR AND GENTLENESS WHICH HE USED TO PROVOKE EACH PERSON LIKE A TRUE EXPERT, UNTIL THEY ABANDONED ALL RESISTANCE, REDISCOVERING THE COURSE OF THEIR EMOTIONS AND EXPRESSING IN WORDS OR TEARS TRAUMAS THAT WERE OFTEN VERY OLD AND HAD BEEN COMPLETELY REMOVED FROM THEIR CONSCIOUSNESS. THIS HORSE WAS A REAL PROFESSOR AND SEEMED TO HAVE AN IMMENSE SPIRIT, WHOSE SPECIAL LIGHT GAVE EACH OF HIS ACTIONS A RESONANCE AND A WEIGHT THAT I WILL NEVER FORGET. OBSERVING HIM IN ACTION, WITH ONE PATIENT AFTER ANOTHER, WOULD HAVE CONSTITUTED AN IDEAL COURSE FOR PSYCHOLOGY STUDENTS AND PSYCHOTHERAPISTS ALIKE. IN MY SUBCONSCIOUS I ALREADY KNEW IT: EVER SINCE THE TIME OF MY CHILDHOOD SPENT ALONGSIDE HORSES AND MY FIRST PHOTOGRAPHS OF THEM, I HAVE ALWAYS FELT THAT MEN CAN DO FAR MORE THAN RIDE HORSES AND THAT THEIR SENSITIVITY TO THE ENVIRONMENT, UNCONSCIOUS AND EVEN MYSTIC SPHERES IS A GIFT TO US. HOWEVER, FROM THAT DAY ON I HAVE SEEN THEM THROUGH DIFFERENT EYES.

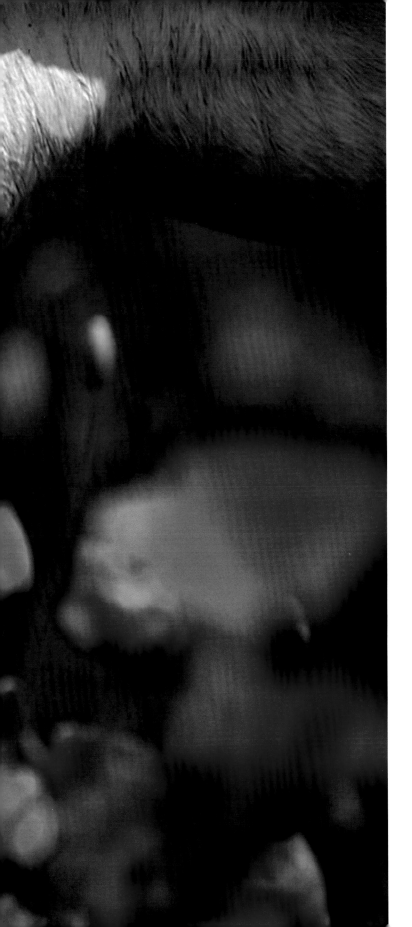

238-239 Amid the poppies, the delicate and fast-moving nose of this handsome Spanish stallion manages to pick out the grass he is seeking. Horses select the plants that they eat with surprising accuracy, but this ability is essential for their survival in a habitat where many grasses and shrubs are highly poisonous for their delicate constitution.

239 This purebred Arabian is eating his fill of the seeds borne on the top of the tall grasses. He instinctively knows that these plants provide far more fat and protein than can be found in cut grass.

sensitivity and fragility

240   For this Haflinger stallion, exploring a new area means setting off
for an adventure, with potential dangers of all kinds. He proceeds
cautiously, senses honed, looking out for hazardous terrain, such as holes
in the ground, or other animals that could suddenly appear, like
predators.

240-241   The modern horse has been shaped by 60 million years of
evolution. Despite domestication and man's protection for over 5000
years, the status of prey is still deeply rooted in this animal, which spends
hours scrutinizing its surroundings, as this Lusitano stallion is doing,
in order to try to recognize potential sources of danger.

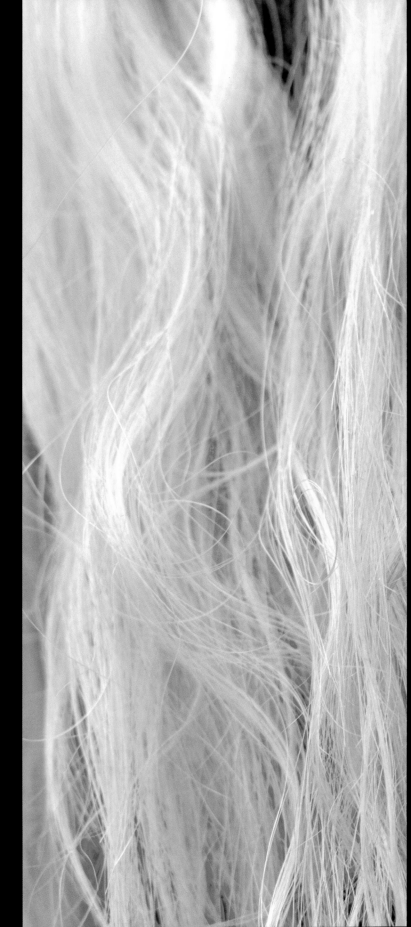

sensitivity and fragility

242-243 Horses' expressions can often be read in their eyes, which are sometimes sad and at others blazing, nostalgic, uneasy or completely vacant. This horse is watching me rather uneasily, asking himself what might be the purpose of the strange device that I am pointing at him.

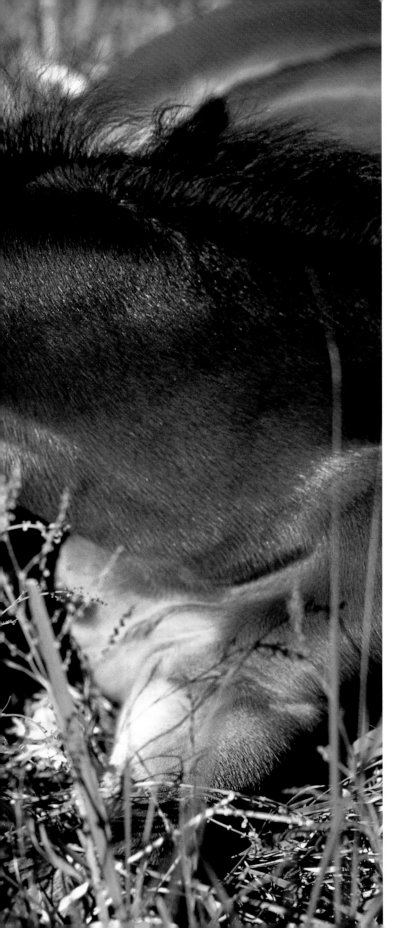

244-245 Foals require frequent rest during their first few weeks of life. They lie down alongside their mothers several times a day and fall into a deep "baby's" sleep, which they will no longer be able to enjoy as adults.

245 This day-old Arabian foal seems surprised at the length of his legs. He already knows how to use them to gallop and even to perform acrobatics, such as kicking or bucking. The energy and speed of foals just a few hours following birth is surprising for us, for our own species takes years to develop a comparable independence of movement. However, it is a matter of survival in the world of the horse: if foals are unable to follow the movements of the herd from their very first hours of life, they will lose its protection and be left to the mercy of predators, such as foxes or condors.

246   Despite the watchfulness of his mother standing next to him, this foal does not feel completely safe. He senses my presence behind him and prepares to rise and move away. Sometimes it takes a while even for domestic foals to develop trust in man. The instinct to flee remains very strong, even after having been handled gently from the very first days.

246-247   This several-week-old Friesian foal seems to be asking himself what he should do. He's trying to assess what sort of danger I might represent and may spring to his feet at any moment. Fortunately, curiosity usually gets the better of fear for most horses.

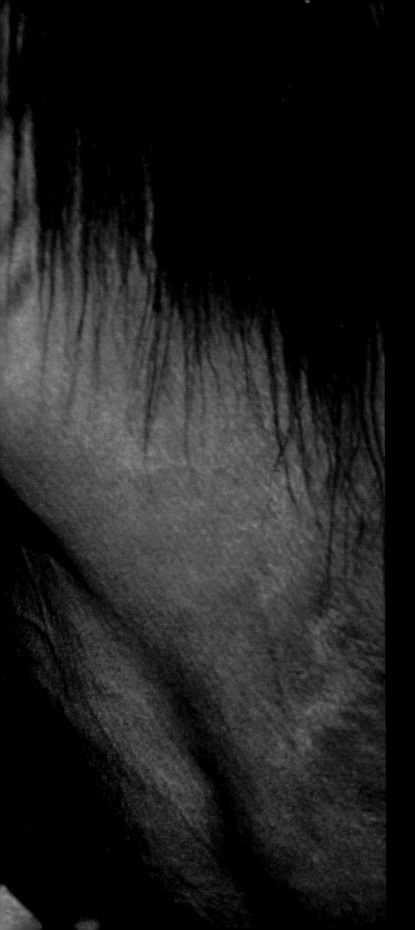

sensitivity and fragility

solidarity and tenderness

solidarity and tenderness

NEVER STAND BETWEEN A MARE AND HER FOAL. IF SHE SHOULD SUDDENLY HAVE THE SENSATION THAT YOU COULD

POSE SOME SORT OF DANGER TO HER BABY, SHE'LL FLATTEN HER EARS AND THREATEN YOU WITH BARED TEETH. IN THIS

CASE, YOU SHOULD GET OUT OF HER REACH AS QUICKLY AS POSSIBLE, ALLOWING HER TO JOIN HER FOAL; OTHERWISE

YOU'LL BE IN FOR A SERIES OF DEEP AND PAINFUL BITES.

THE WHOLE HERD PROTECTS EACH MEMBER OF THE FAMILY, AS I'VE HAD THE CHANCE TO WITNESS ON SEVERAL OC-

CASIONS. I WAS ONCE IN THE SWAMPY MAREMMA AREA OF TUSCANY, WHERE HORSES THAT HAVE NEVER SEEN A STA-

BLE ROAM FREE. IT WAS A SPRING MORNING, BEFORE THE SUN HAD RISEN, AND I WAS BARELY ABLE TO MAKE OUT THE

SURPRISING SCENE OF A YOUNG MARE THAT HAD JUST GIVEN BIRTH TO HER FIRST FOAL. THE WET AND BEWILDERED

FOAL WAS NOT YET ABLE TO STAND ON HIS LONG, SLENDER LEGS AND HIS MOTHER WAS LYING ALONGSIDE HIM TO RE-

COVER FROM THE EXERTION. IN THIS WILD AREA, THIS IS THE IDEAL MOMENT FOR THE ATTACK OF CARNIVORES. IN THE

MAREMMA FOXES OFTEN TAKE ADVANTAGE OF MOMENTS OF VULNERABILITY, AS DO PUMAS, WOLVES AND VULTURES

ELSEWHERE. HORSES THAT ARE VERY OLD, SICK OR TOO YOUNG TO DEFEND THEMSELVES ARE ENTICING PREY. HOW-

EVER, THESE ANIMALS ARE PROTECTED BY THE SOLIDARITY OF THE OTHERS. ON THIS OCCASION, THE HERD WAS

ARRANGED IN A CIRCLE AROUND THE YOUNG MOTHER AND HER FOAL.

EACH HORSE WAS POSITIONED IN SUCH A WAY TO ENABLE IT TO STAND WATCH AND PREVENT ATTACKS OF ANY

KIND. THE MAGICAL CIRCLE EXUDED A SENSE OF PEACE, GENTLENESS AND HARMONY THAT I WILL NEVER FORGET. THE

GROUP HAD INTERVENED FOR ONE OF ITS MEMBERS, SILENTLY, CALMLY AND VERY NATURALLY. THIS ATTENTION TO THE

FOALS IS ALSO THE RESPONSIBILITY OF THE HERD AND NOT JUST THE MARE, AS IS EASILY CONFIRMED. WHEN I WAS PHOTOGRAPHING HERDS OF 500 TO 800 HORSES IN ARGENTINA, I NOTICED HOW THE GROUP MANAGES TO PROTECT THE FOALS. THE ADULTS POSITIONED THEMSELVES SO THAT THE YOUNGSTERS WERE NEVER AT THE BACK OR ON THE SIDES OF THE GROUP. THE FOALS WERE ALWAYS PUSHED TOWARD THE CENTER AND PROTECTED BY THE ADULTS THAT SURROUNDED THEM.

I'D ALREADY HAD THE CHANCE TO OBSERVE DEMONSTRATIONS OF SOLIDARITY, ESPECIALLY BETWEEN MOTHER AND DAUGHTER. IN PARTICULAR, WHEN A MARE ASSISTS HER DAUGHTER AT THE BIRTH OF HER FIRST FOALS, AND SHARES THE RESPONSIBILITY OF WATCHING OVER AND EDUCATING THE YOUNGSTERS, AS THOUGH THE OLDER HORSE WISHED TO TEACH THE NOVICE THE RULES OF THIS ART. HOWEVER, THE OPPOSITE IS ALSO TRUE. INDEED, WHEN AN ELDERLY MARE HAS A HYPERACTIVE FOAL THAT REQUIRES MUCH ENERGY, I'VE SEEN DAUGHTERS ASSUME THE CARE OF THEIR STEPBROTHER AS WELL AS THEIR OWN FOALS IN ORDER TO ALLOW THEIR MOTHER TO REST A LITTLE.

WE OFTEN DON'T REALIZE HOW TIRING A FOAL CAN BE FOR ITS MOTHER, BUT IT SUCKLES SEVERAL TIMES EACH HOUR, PLAYS CONSTANTLY AND FOOLS AROUND, REQUIRING CONTINUOUS WATCHING DURING THE FIRST FEW WEEKS OF LIFE. SUBSEQUENTLY IT BECOMES LESS DEPENDENT, BUT STILL NEEDS MUCH ATTENTION FROM ITS MOTHER.

251   Two young horses sniff each other on their first encounter.

252 left   A close relationship between two young horses.

252 center   A mare fiercely defends her foal, which has taken refuge next to her.

252 right   Two Haflinger friends in the mountain pastures.

253   Solidarity is not a sentiment restricted to mares and their foals: stallions protect their offspring too.

solidarity and tenderness

ALTHOUGH BREEDERS COMPLETELY SEVER THE TIES BETWEEN MARE AND FOAL AFTER SIX MONTHS, THE CLOSE BOND PERSISTS FOR MUCH LONGER IN NATURE, WHERE FOALS STAY WITH THEIR MOTHERS UNTIL THE ARRIVAL OF THE NEXT ONE, THE FOLLOWING YEAR. ALTHOUGH THE MARES WILL THEN SPEND MOST OF THEIR TIME CARING FOR THE NEW AR- RIVAL, THEY WILL CONTINUE TO MAINTAIN A VERY CLOSE RELATIONSHIP WITH THEIR OLDER OFFSPRING. IF POSSIBLE, THEY OFTEN STAY WITH HER FOR ALL HER LIFE, DEMONSTRATING THEIR AFFECTION AND KEEPING THIS FILIAL BOND ALIVE.

YOU NEED ONLY TO LOOK AT THE EXCHANGE BETWEEN A MARE AND HER FOAL TO REALIZE THAT THIS GREAT LOVE CANNOT SUDDENLY DISAP- PEAR WITH WEANING. I AM DEEPLY TOUCHED EACH TIME I SEE THE TEN- DERNESS WITH WHICH A MARE LICKS HER NEWBORN FOAL AND THE GEN- TLENESS WITH WHICH SHE NUDGES IT WITH HER NOSE TO HELP IT TO STAND AND DIRECTS IT TOWARD HER UDDER TO SUCKLE. THE GAZE THAT SHE DIRECTS AT HER FOAL IS BRIMMING WITH MATERNAL LOVE.

HOWEVER, SOLIDARITY BETWEEN HORSES IS NOT JUST A COMMUNITY AND FAMILY MATTER, BUT ALSO INVOLVES INDIVIDUALS WITH A SPECIAL AFFINITY. FRIENDSHIPS BETWEEN HORSES ARE VERY STRONG AND IN- CREDIBLY DURABLE. THEY USUALLY LAST A WHOLE LIFETIME, ESPECIALLY

AMONG MARES, AND ARE OFTEN VERY SYMBIOTIC. IN TERMS OF DAILY LIFE, THIS CAN BE SEEN IN THE EXCHANGE OF AFFECTIONATE GESTURES, MASSAGES AND SESSIONS SPENT STANDING HEAD-TO-TAIL IN ORDER TO SWISH THE FLIES AWAY FROM THE OTHER'S HEAD.

ALTHOUGH THIS MAY SEEM INSIGNIFICANT, IT IS ACTUALLY A TRUE FORM OF SOLIDARITY, BECAUSE FLIES ARE TERRIBLY IRRITATING FOR HORSES. SIMILARLY, RECIPROCAL MASSAGES ALSO APPEAR EXTREMELY IMPORTANT. THESE ARE NOT PERFORMED CASUALLY OR MECHANICALLY, BUT IN AREAS OF GREAT TENSION OR IRRITATION, AND THUS PAIN, WHICH THE HORSE IS UNABLE TO REACH ALONE. ANIMAL BEHAVIORISTS HAVE NOTED THAT THIS RITUAL NOT ONLY ALLOWS THE RESOLUTION OF LA- TENT CONFLICT BETWEEN INDIVIDUALS, BUT ALSO GENERATES PHYSICAL WELL-BEING. INDEED, WHEN HORSES MASSAGE EACH OTHER, THEIR HEARTBEAT SLOWS DOWN, PRODUCING A STRONG LONG-LASTING CALM- ING EFFECT.

EACH FRIENDSHIP IS UNIQUE. IT'S NOT TRUE THAT HORSES WILL MAKE FRIENDS WITH ANYONE, FOR THEY TOO HAVE "LOVE-AT-FIRST-SIGHT" RE- LATIONSHIPS, TENDER FEELINGS AND ANIMOSITIES, WHICH CAN SOME- TIMES BE VERY DEEP. A COUPLE OF HORSES THAT DISLIKE EACH OTHER ARE CAPABLE OF REMAINING COMPLETELY INDIFFERENT TO EACH OTHER,

AT THE OPPOSITE ENDS OF A FIELD, FOR YEARS. ON THE OTHER HAND, SOME FRIENDSHIPS ARE FORGED IMMEDIATELY, ALTHOUGH A FEW DAYS ARE ALWAYS NEEDED FOR ABSOLUTE TRUST. AFTER THIS PERIOD THE TWO ANIMALS WILL LIVE IN COMPLETE SYMBIOSIS, GRAZING NOSE-TO-NOSE, SLEEPING SHOULDER-TO-SHOULDER, AND WHISKING AWAY THE FLIES AND SCRATCHING EACH OTHER IN THE HEAD-TAIL POSITION. THEY WATCH THE WORLD WITH FOUR EYES, GENERALLY TURNING THEIR HEADS IN EXACTLY THE SAME DIRECTION AND WITH THE SAME MOVE-MENT. THEY CEASELESSLY CARESS EACH OTHER WITH THEIR NOSES AND CALL EACH OTHER DESPERATELY IF, BY SOME MISFORTUNE, THEY HAP-PEN TO BE SEPARATED.

IT TOOK ME A LONG TIME TO REALIZE IT, BUT A FRIENDSHIP IS NEVER ACTUALLY REPLACED BY ANOTHER. EACH IS UNIQUE AND THE STRONGEST ONES ARE IRREPLACEABLE AND UNSWERVING. SOMETIMES OLD FRIENDS MAY MEET AGAIN AFTER YEARS OF SEPARATION, AND THEIR REUNION IS A VERY TOUCHING SCENE. MORE SURPRISING STILL, I'VE NOTICED HOW SEPARATED FRIENDS MISS EACH OTHER. THEY SEEK EACH OTHER FOR MONTHS AND YEARS, ALWAYS HOPING TO FIND EACH OTHER. MY HORSE HAD ENJOYED A GREAT FRIENDSHIP WITH A GRAY MARE FOR FIVE OR SIX YEARS. HOWEVER, AFTER THIS TIME I DECIDED TO CHANGE STABLES SO THAT I COULD FINALLY HAVE HIM NEAR HOME. WHEN HE REALIZED THAT HE WAS LEAVING FOR GOOD, HE NOT ONLY WENT BERSERK IN THE VAN THAT WAS TRANSPORTING HIM, LASHING OUT IN ALL DIRECTIONS, BUT THEN FELL INTO A STATE OF DEEP DE-PRESSION AND DESPONDENCY. ONCE HE ARRIVED AT HIS DESTINATION, HE FELL ILL FOR MONTHS, DESPITE HAVING ALWAYS HAD AN IRON CON-STITUTION. HIS FRIEND MISSED HIM AND THE FEELING WAS RECIPROCAL. A FEW MONTHS LATER THE RIDER AND FRIEND WHO LOOKED AFTER HIS FORMER FIELD MATE TOLD ME THAT TO HER GREAT ASTONISHMENT HER MARE STILL CONTINUED TO SEEK MY CHESTNUT GELDING. EACH TIME THAT SHE SAW A REDDISH HORSE, SHE'D EAGERLY RAISE HER HEAD, WIDEN HER EYES, SNIFF THE AIR WITH HER DILATED NOSTRILS AND CALL OUT WITH A NEIGH, BEFORE REALIZING HER MISTAKE AND RETURNING TO HER WORK DEJECTEDLY.

HORSES DISPLAY GREAT SOLIDARITY AND TENDERNESS TOWARD OTHERS OF THE GROUP, BUT SOMETIMES ALSO TOWARD MAN. IF YOU BELIEVE IN THEM AND DESERVE THEM, THEN THEY WILL WILLINGLY SERVE YOU, FULFILLING ALL YOUR NEEDS, WITH NEVER A THOUGHT FOR THEIR OWN WELL-BEING. IT IS TRUE TO SAY THAT THESE HORSES, READY TO RISE TO ANY CHALLENGE, HAVE GREAT HEARTS. HOWEVER, IT IS A

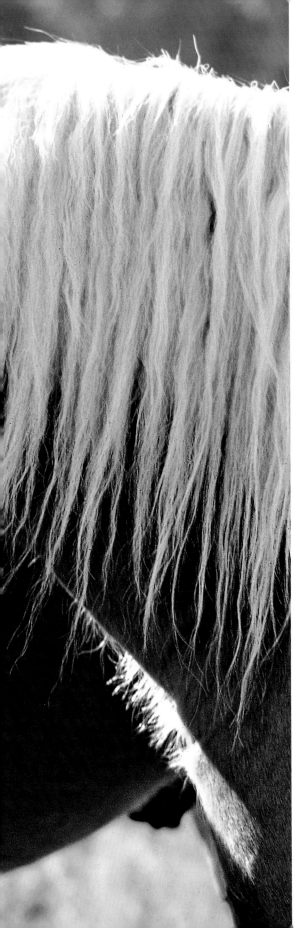

254 During a foal's first few days of life, the mare sniffs him very frequently, as though impregnating herself with his smell and ensuring that it really is him. Indeed, it is principally the sense of smell that enables her to identify him among the many foals of the herd, which often closely resemble each other.

256-257 Two horses that haven't met before approach to smell each other. Their first contact often takes the form of blowing onto each other's nostrils.

259 This little Icelandic pony, just a few days old, follows his mother as best he can, always staying close to her in order to benefit from her protection.

GREAT UNDERSTATEMENT, FOR THESE NATURALLY PRUDENT CREATURES ARE WILLING TO COVER HUNDREDS OF MILES WITH US ON THEIR BACKS, JUMP OBSTACLES HIGHER THAN THEMSELVES, AND GALLOP ENDLESSLY, SIMPLY FOR OUR PLEASURE. EVER SINCE THE TIMES OF THE CAVALRY, THOSE WHO FOUGHT ALONGSIDE HORSES BROUGHT BACK STORIES OF ALL KINDS FROM THE FRONT. WHETHER TRUE OR IMAGINARY, THEY NONETHELESS BEAR AN UNCANNY RESEMBLANCE TO EACH OTHER OVER THE AGES AND ACROSS DIFFERENT CIVILIZATIONS, AND CONSEQUENTLY MUST HAVE SOME FACTUAL BASIS. THEY TELL OF HORSES THAT FOUGHT TO PROTECT THEIR RIDERS, WITH WHOM THEY STAYED IF THEY FELL, AND OF ANIMALS CAPABLE OF CONTINUING THE CHARGE WITH A WOUNDED OR EVEN DEAD RIDER ON THEIR BACK. HISTORY IS PERVADED BY THE LEGENDARY BOND BETWEEN CERTAIN FAMOUS MEN AND THEIR HORSES, SUCH AS ALEXANDER THE GREAT AND BUCEPHALUS OR NAPOLEON AND MARENGO.

THE BOND BETWEEN HORSES AND MEN ALSO HAS ITS FAIR SHARE OF MYSTERY. INDEED, CERTAIN PEOPLE MANAGE TO BE ADOPTED BY HORSES AS MEMBERS OF THE HERD, AND ARE CONSIDERED AND LOVED LIKE MEMBERS OF THE FAMILY. THIS KIND OF RELATIONSHIP MAY ALSO BE ESTABLISHED IN THE ABSENCE OF THE HERD WITH A SINGLE HORSE IN A

solidarity and tenderness

STABLE. THIS IS PARTICULARLY TRUE FOR STALLIONS, WHICH EASILY DEVELOP A SENSE OF RESPONSIBILITY AND PROTECTION TOWARD THEIR RIDERS OR OWNERS, FOR THIS IS THE NATURAL ROLE THAT THEY WOULD PLAY IN THE HERD.

THE HORSE'S SENSE OF RESPONSIBILITY BECOMES EVEN STRONGER WHEN THE RIDER IS A FRAGILE PERSON. THIS RELATIONSHIP CAN BE CLEARLY SEEN WITH PHYSICALLY HANDICAPPED RIDERS OR CHILDREN. MOST HORSES ARE PARTICULARLY CAREFUL, GENTLE AND ATTENTIVE TOWARD A DISABLED, INEXPERIENCED OR SIMPLY UNWITTING COMPANION. ON COUNTLESS OCCASIONS I HAVE SEEN HORSES "CATCH" A RIDER WHO HAS LOST HIS BALANCE, SWERVING TO PLACE THEMSELVES FIRMLY BENEATH HIS WAVERING BODY. THEY ARE ALSO ABLE TO AVOID A DOG OR CHILD THAT HAS WANDERED ALMOST BENEATH THEIR HOOVES, LOWER THEIR HEAD TO ENABLE YOUNG RIDERS TO PLACE THE BIT IN THEIR MOUTH, OR WAIT PATIENTLY ALONGSIDE THEM IF THEY FALL AND NEED TO REMOUNT. EVEN PARTICULARLY LIVELY AND HIGHLY-STRUNG HORSES BECOME AS MEEK AS LAMBS IF A CHILD IS PLACED ON THEIR BACK. THEY WALK SLOWLY, AS THOUGH ON EGGSHELLS, TOLERATING THE LITTLE SQUEALS – OF JOY OR FRIGHT – THE FLAPPING LEGS AND THE TUGS AT THE BIT. IN SHORT, THEY PUT UP WITH EVERYTHING THAT THEY WOULD NEVER TOLERATE FROM THEIR USUAL RIDER.

WHEN I WAS SIX OR SEVEN YEARS OLD I WAS "ADOPTED" BY A DRAFT MARE. SHE LIVED ALONE IN A FIELD OPPOSITE MY HOUSE. OUR RECIPROCAL SOLITUDE THREW US TOGETHER AND THE RESULT WAS A TRULY GREAT LOVE STORY.

I CALLED HER CÂLINE (CUDDLES) AND SHE ADOPTED ME WHOLEHEARTEDLY. SHE'D ALLOW ME TO LEAP BETWEEN HER HEAVY HOOVES, JUMP ONTO HER BACK FROM THE BRANCH OF A TREE, PLAIT HER MANE AND BEDECK HER WITH PIGTAILS THAT WOULD HAVE BEEN THE ENVY OF MY ABANDONED DOLLS. SHE WOULD CALM MY ANXIETY AND WORRIES BY BLOWING GENTLY THROUGH MY HAIR, SATISFY MY IMAGINATIVE WHIMS BY RACING WITH ME, AND ROCK ME WHEN I HELD HER HEAVY HEAD IN MY CHILD'S ARMS.

CÂLINE WOULD IMPATIENTLY AWAIT MY RETURN FROM SCHOOL AND, WHEN THE CAR FINALLY TURNED INTO THE STREET, SHE'D CROSS THE FIELD AT A GALLOP.

I WOULD STAY WITH HER ALMOST UNTIL DINNERTIME, FOR ENDLESS CARESSES. THEN, WHEN DARKNESS FELL, SHE WOULD WAIT BENEATH THE WINDOWS OF MY BEDROOM TO WISH ME GOODNIGHT WHEN I CLOSED THE SHUTTERS. HOWEVER, ONE DAY I RETURNED FROM SCHOOL TO FIND CÂLINE HAD DISAPPEARED, AND HER FIELD WAS EMPTY. I SCOURED THE AREA FOR MILES AROUND FOR MANY MONTHS, BUT IN VAIN. MANY YEARS LATER I REALIZED THAT MY ADOPTED MOTHER HAD BEEN SOLD FOR MEAT, BY THE POUND. IF THE BUTCHER WEIGHED ALL THE LOVE THAT SHE HAD IN HER HEART, THEN HE MUST HAVE PAID DEARLY FOR HER.

A MEAT HORSE GAVE ME ALL THE TENDERNESS AND LOVE IN THE WORLD: THE LOVE OF A MOTHER, A SISTER AND A FRIEND. SHE NOT ONLY FILLED MY CHILDHOOD WITH JOY, BUT MY WHOLE EXISTENCE, GIVING ME MY LIFELONG LOVE OF HORSES.

260-261 Living in a herd is a form of protection for horses. Each individual monitors its surroundings and alerts the others in case of danger: if attacked by predators, they can defend themselves better by joining forces. The weaker members of the herd, such as the foals, are often placed in the center of the group, and the stallion stops every now and then to ensure that none of the animals have got lost or have been left behind.

solidarity and tenderness

262-263 and 263 Horses, particurarly if they are friends, spend long moments scratching and massaging each other. This enables them to alleviate itching and tension in those spots that they are unable to reach themselves. It is also a gesture of friendship that calms them, and it has been demonstrated that their heartbeat slows significantly during "grooming," as this behavior is termed.

solidarity and tenderness

266 In the wild, the mare and her foal maintain an affectionate and protective relationship long after weaning. This mare is about to give birth to a new foal, but the one born the previous spring will continue to stay with her. This special relationship between mother and foal can last a lifetime.

266-267 Following puberty, around the age of 18 months, this group of young horses was excluded from the herd, composed of mares and a stallion. The animals join forces in order to protect each other until adulthood, when each will gradually find a place in a new herd: the females as brood mares and the males as stallions.

268-269   It is essential for horses to be able to touch and caress each other. If they could rank the things that are most important to them, their social life would be at the top of the list, above their freedom even, for a big field is never worth as much as a good companion. A solitary life is equivalent to mere survival for horses.

solidarity and tenderness

270-271   Certain horses live in very close proximity to each other within the same herd, and may also stay together when on the move. Others, however, refuse each other and always keep a respectful distance, such as the horse on the left here, which moves away from the two friends walking toward each other in the center.

272 Friendship does not prevent relations of dominance from being established. When a horse is dominant over another, it may display highly authoritarian behavior, nipping its subordinate, as shown here, to oblige the animal to obey it, or threatening it with flattened ears. Although this behavior may seem rather tyrannical to us, both animals actually live in perfect harmony, each knowing its place and almost always inseparable from the other.

273 Friendships between horses are often exclusive, but these young Icelandic ponies are fairly open, due chiefly to their tender age.

274-275   The meeting and beginning of a friendship between two Connemara foals in Ireland. Relations between horses are almost always extremely pacific and friendly.

276 and 277 Horses use their noses both to smell and to touch, and these functions are also essential for getting to know their peers. Indeed, their sense of smell enables them to recognize other horses when they meet again, in the same way that foals identify their mothers.

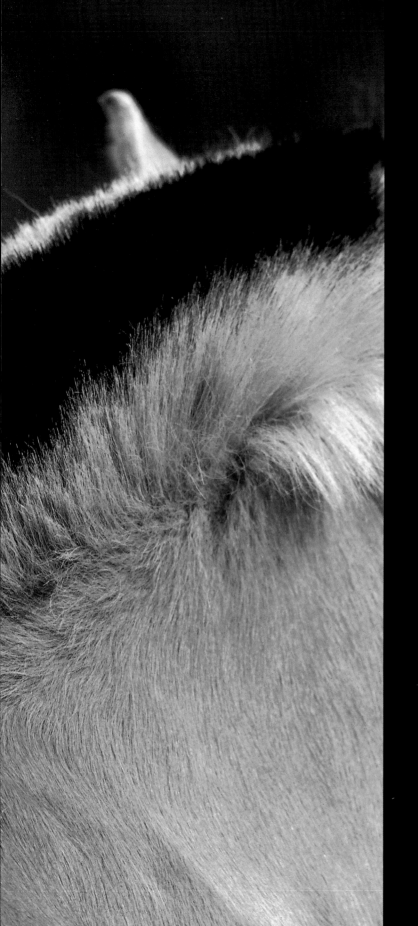

solidarity and tenderness

278-279   This Norwegian Fjord stallion tries to reassure his companion and win her favor by scratching her withers. He will need to be very gentle and persevering in order to attain his goal!

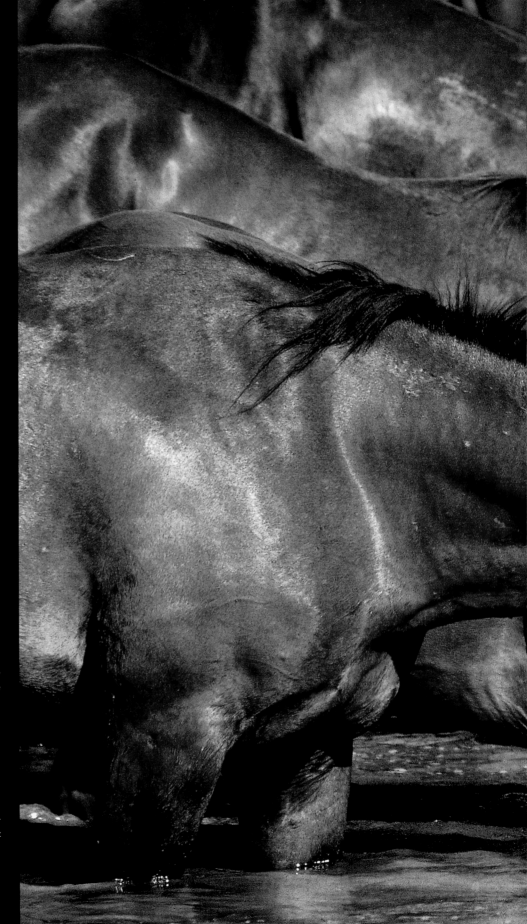

280-281 There is no sense of property among horses. They peacefully divide the resources available to them, in this case the water of a river. The same is true at pasture, where someone could try to graze the best part or certain kinds of grass. However, not horses: sharing is perfectly natural for them. On the other hand, when food is rationed in the stables, they sometimes unashamedly steal their neighbor's meager meal.

282-283 The tranquility and power of these great herds is unnerving. This group of Argentinian Criollos moves around the pampas without any of its members being abandoned or attacked. Dozens of horses become one, in a huge mass that ripples to the rhythm of their rumps and vibrates to the sound of their hooves that drum the ground.

284-285　A foal's attachment to its mother, expressed in many affectionate gestures, is always a very touching sight, like this foal rubbing his head against his mother's belly. However, his mother is not only his source of tender loving care, but also knows how to reprimand him (with a little nip) and forbid him from doing certain things, such as straying too far from her side.

286-287   This little Icelandic pony foal is resting for a few minutes by his mother, who always remains by him while he sleeps, ensuring that no one approaches.

287   Even when sleeping, horses continue to display their solidarity. While one slumbers, the other keeps watch alongside, ensuring that they are not taken by surprise by danger of any kind. They then swap roles, so that both can rest without risking being attacked while sleeping.

288-289   I never fail to be moved by the sweetness of foals. Each birth in my stables is a celebration and a source of joy and marvel that is constantly renewed.

289   This foal, taken away from his mother to be photographed, calls her with shrill neighs and rushes toward her. He feels threatened and hurries to seek her protection.

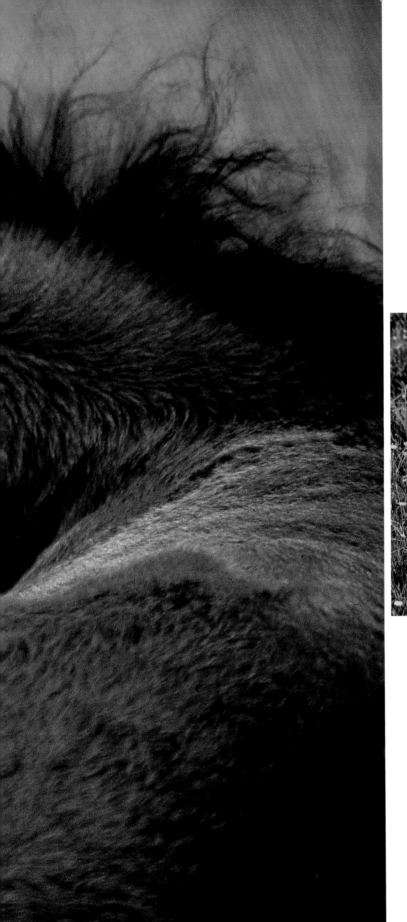

290-291 and 291   When I photograph foals, I spend hours in the field, caressing the mother and then sitting and waiting for the uneasiness to pass. Then I gradually crawl toward the foals. They do not run away, but usually keep an eye on what I'm doing. However, some approach me and want to nibble at my hair, clothes and camera. Their different characters are already clearly discernible.

292-293 and 293   Mares lick their foals clean following birth, not only removing the amniotic fluid, but also warming them and reviving them after their grueling ordeal. Although this particular gesture subsequently becomes less common, mares ceaselessly touch and sniff their foals, as though reinforcing the bond established during the first few moments of their offspring's life.

294 and 295   A foal's mother is not only an endless source of affection and attention, but also its principal teacher and sole model. A foal relies heavily on observation and imitation of its mother's behavior in order to learn how to choose the right grass to graze and to behave appropriately with other horses or species. This explains why foals often closely resemble their mothers in both behavior and character, which are determined by imitation to at least the same degree as purely genetic factors.

296-297   All the tenderness and trust in the world transpire from this Haflinger mare and her foal, born the previous evening. The foal regains its strength by sleeping and suckling several times an hour, but when awake, it is already able to gallop and kick like an adult.

298-299   Friendships between horses are blind to both breed and size, and are merely a matter of affinity of character. The most surprising thing about these two friends, who closely resemble Oliver and Hardy, is that the little pony is the dominant one and displays very authoritarian behavior toward his gentle-natured companion.

300   Beauty, elegance, pride, great sensitivity and even sensuality
constitute the essence of the horse: a concentrate of power streaked
with fear and tenderness. How can anyone fail to fall deeply in love
with these animals?

Cover   The feverish intensity of the horse's gaze,
the graceful movement of its neck, its finely chiseled ears and
velvety soft quivering nostrils all convey its sensitivity, untamed power
and fragility.

Gabriele Boiselle

After working for a few years as a journalist, Gabrielle Boiselle
returned to her two first loves: photography and horses. In
1984 she published her first calendar, illustrated with splendid
photos of Arabian horses. Her exceptional artistic sensitivity
combined with an impeccable technique have made the
German photographer famous: she is now one
of the world's most renowned artist in the challenging and very
special sphere of equine photography.

Agnès Galletier

Journalist, writer and horse lover, Agnès Galletier continues
to pay tribute to these magnificent animals with her books,
striving to enable the public at large to understand them
better, and thus love them. She has published many works
in conjunction with Gabrielle Boiselle, particularly in France.